THINK

STUDENT'S BOOK STARTER A1

Herbert Puchta, Jeff Stranks & Peter Lewis-Jones

CAMBRIDGE
UNIVERSITY PRESS

CONTENTS

	FUNCTIONS & SPEAKING	GRAMMAR	VOCABULARY
Unit 1 **One world** p 12	Getting to know someone Talking about yourself and others	Question words *to be*	Countries and nationalities Adjectives
Unit 2 **I feel happy** p 20	Talking about feelings Asking questions Expressing likes and dislikes	*to be* (negative, singular and plural) *to be* (questions and short answers) Object pronouns	Adjectives to describe feelings Positive and negative adjectives

	FUNCTIONS & SPEAKING	GRAMMAR	VOCABULARY
Unit 3 **Me and my family** p 30	Describing good qualities Talking about family Paying compliments	Possessive *'s* Possessive adjectives *this / that / these / those*	Family members House and furniture
Unit 4 **In the city** p 38	Talking about places in a town/city Giving directions Buying in a shop	*there is / there are* *some / any* Imperatives	Places in a town/city Prepositions of place Numbers 100+ Prices

	FUNCTIONS & SPEAKING	GRAMMAR	VOCABULARY
Unit 5 **In my free time** p 48	Talking about habits and activities Talking about technology habits Encouraging someone	Present simple Adverbs of frequency Present simple (negative and questions)	Free-time activities Gadgets
Unit 6 **Friends** p 56	Helping a friend Describing people	*have / has got* (positive, negative and questions) Countable and uncountable nouns	Parts of the body Describing people

PRONUNCIATION	THINK	SKILLS	
/h/ or /w/ in question words	**Values:** The Olympic Spirit **Self-esteem:** The 'Me' flag	**Reading**	Website: Mad about The Olympics
			Dialogue: Favourite football teams
			Photostory: Just a little joke
		Listening	Radio quiz: The One-Minute Challenge
		Writing	Completing a questionnaire: Personal information
Vowel sounds – adjectives	**Values:** Welcoming a new classmate **Train to Think:** Categorising	**Reading**	Text messages: Hi there!
			Dialogue: Deciding what to do
			Culture: Masks from around the world
		Listening	Dialogues: Talking about feelings
		Writing	Text message: Describing feelings and things
this / that / these / those	**Values:** Families **Self-esteem:** Being part of a family	**Reading**	Article: Kate Middleton
			Dialogue: Agata's family
			Photostory: A song for Ruby
		Listening	Dialogues: Describing family
		Writing	Description: Your favourite room
Word stress in numbers	**Values:** My town/city **Train to Think:** Exploring numbers	**Reading**	Brochure: Window of the World
			Dialogues: In the shops
			Culture: Parks around the world
		Listening	Dialogues: Asking for directions
		Writing	Brochure: A brochure for your town / city
Present simple verbs – third person	**Values:** Better together or better alone? **Self-esteem:** What makes me happy?	**Reading**	Newsletter: I love Glee club!
			Quiz: Does TV control your life?
			Photostory: The school play
		Listening	Monologues: Describing electronic gadgets
		Writing	Paragraph: Days in your life
Long vowel sound /eɪ/	**Values:** Helping a friend **Train to Think:** Attention to detail	**Reading**	Article: A real friend
			Dialogue: A surprise for Olivia
			Culture: Welcoming people around the world
		Listening	Interview: Friendship bands
		Writing	Paragraph: Describing a friend

WELCOME

The alphabet

Aa Bb Cc Dd

Ee Ff Gg Hh

Ii Jj Kk Ll

Mm Nn Oo

Pp Qq Rr Ss

Tt Uu Vv Ww

Xx Yy Zz

1 🔊 1.02 Listen to the alphabet. Then listen again and repeat.

2 🔊 1.03 Listen to the sounds and repeat.

/eɪ/	/iː/	/e/	/aɪ/	/əʊ/	/uː/	/ɑː/
a h j k	b c d e g p t v	f l m n s x z	i y	o	q u w	r

3 SPEAKING Work in pairs. Spell your name to your partner. Your partner writes your name. Is he/she correct?

Colours

1 Write the colours in the correct places in the key.

black | blue | brown | green | grey | orange
pink | purple | red | ~~white~~ | yellow

Key

1 _white_	7 _____
2 _____	8 _____
3 _____	9 _____
4 _____	10 _____
5 _____	11 _____
6 _____	

2 SPEAKING Work in pairs. What colours can you see around you? Tell your partner.

A

B

C *1*

D

E

F

G

H

I

J

K

L

M

N

O

P

International words

1 Match the words in the list with the pictures. Write 1–16 in the boxes.

1 airport | 2 bus | 3 café
4 city | 5 football | 6 hamburger
7 hotel | 8 phone | 9 pizza
10 restaurant | 11 sandwich
12 sushi | 13 taxi | 14 television
15 tablet | 16 wi-fi

2 🔊 1.04 Listen, check and repeat.

3 SPEAKING Work in pairs. Choose one of the words in Exercise 1 and spell it to your partner. He/She writes the word. Is he/she correct?

Articles: *a* and *an*

1 Match the sentences in the list with the pictures. Write 1–4 in the boxes.

1 It's a blue football.

2 It's an orange football.

3 It's a red football.

4 It's a black and white football.

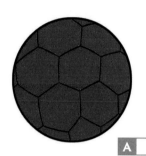
A [ ]

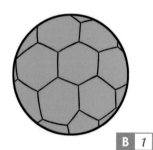
B [*1*]

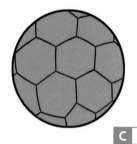
C [ ]

D [ ]

2 Write *a* or *an*.

0 ___*an*___ airport

1 _____ Italian restaurant

2 _____ red bus

3 _____ sandwich

4 _____ yellow taxi

5 _____ orange phone

6 _____ American football player

7 _____ famous actor

The day

1 Write the words in the list under the pictures.

afternoon | ~~evening~~ | morning | night

_____*evening*_____

_____

_____

_____

Saying *Hello* and *Goodbye*

1 ◀)) 1.05 **Complete the dialogues with the words in the list. Listen and check.**

Bye | Good | have | Hi | How | morning
night | See you | thanks | ~~this~~

1

ANDY   Hello. My name's Andy.

TOM   Hi, Andy. I'm Tom, and ⁰ *this* is Lucy.

LUCY   ¹_____ , Andy.

ANDY   Hi, Tom. Hi, Lucy.

2

ABI   ²_____ afternoon, Mrs Hamilton.

MRS HAMILTON   Hi, Abi. ³_____ are you?

ABI   Great, ⁴_____ . And you?

MRS HAMILTON   I'm fine, thanks.

3

DAVE   Good ⁵_____ , Mr Thomas.

MR THOMAS   Hello, Dave. How are you?

DAVE   I'm fine, thank you.

MR THOMAS   Good. I'll see you in class.

DAVE   ⁶_____ , Mr Thomas.

4

JIM   Bye, Rachel.

RACHEL   Bye, Jim. ⁷_____ later.

JIM   Yeah, ⁸_____ a good day.

5

SUE   Good ⁹_____ , Mum.

MUM   Night, Sue. Sleep well.

Classroom objects

1 Look at the pictures. Do you know these words? If not, ask your teacher: *What's ... in English?*

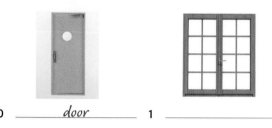

0 _____door_____   1 _____

2 _____   3 _____

4 _____   5 _____

6 _____   7 _____

8 _____   9 _____

2 ◄)) 1.06 Write the words in the list under the pictures in Exercise 1. Listen, check and repeat.

board | book | chair | computer | desk
~~door~~ | pen | pencil | projector | window

3 Are there any other classroom objects you can think of?

4 SPEAKING Work in pairs. Point to the pictures in Exercise 1. Ask and answer questions.

> What's this in English?   It's a desk.

5 SPEAKING Work in pairs. Find things in your classroom and say the colours.

> a red pen   an orange chair

Numbers 0–20

1 ◄)) 1.07 Look at the numbers 0–20. Listen and repeat.

0	zero/'oh'		
1	one	11	eleven
2	two	12	twelve
3	three	13	thirteen
4	four	14	fourteen
5	five	15	fifteen
6	six	16	sixteen
7	seven	17	seventeen
8	eight	18	eighteen
9	nine	19	nineteen
10	ten	20	twenty

2 SPEAKING Work in pairs. Choose three numbers from Exercise 1. Tell a partner to write them. Is he/she right?

3 ◄)) 1.08 Listen and write the phone numbers you hear.

1 _____   3 _____
2 _____   4 _____

4 SPEAKING What's your favourite number? Compare with a partner.

Plural nouns

1 Write the words under the pictures.

0 _two chairs_   1 _____   2 _____

3 _____   4 _____   5 _____

2 Match the singular and plural nouns.

Singular		Plural	
0	one man	*b*	a	three people
1	one woman		b	four men
2	one person		c	six children
3	one child		d	five women

Classroom language

1 🔊 1.09 **Listen and number the phrases in the order you hear them. Write 1–10 in the boxes.**

☐ a Open your books.

☐ c Put your hand up.

☐ e What does this mean?

☐ g That's right.

1 i Close your books.

2 🔊 1.10 **Listen again and repeat.**

☐ b Listen!

☐ d Look at the picture.

☐ f Sorry, I don't understand.

☐ h That's wrong.

☐ j Work with a partner.

Numbers 20–100

1 🔊 1.11 **Match the numbers with the words. Listen and check.**

a	20			fifty
b	30			eighty
c	40			ninety
d	50			seventy
e	60			one hundred
f	70			thirty
g	80		*a*	twenty
h	90			sixty
i	100			forty

> **LOOK!**
> 33 = thirty-three   56 = fifty-six   97 = ninety-seven

2 🔊 1.12 **How do you say these numbers? Listen, check and repeat.**

1	24	4	49	7	74
2	87	5	54	8	95
3	33	6	62		

3 **Write the numbers.**

0	24	*twenty-four*
1	47	_____
2	60	_____
3	89	_____
4	30	_____
5	58	_____
6	72	_____
7	91	_____

Messages

1 🔊 1.13 **Read and listen to the message. Complete the message to Liam.**

Hi, Liam,

Message from Oliver Holmes.

His house number is [1] _____.

The bus number is [2] _____.

His phone number is [3] _____.

2 🔊 1.14 **Now listen and complete the message to Abi.**

Hi, Abi,

Message from Mrs Davis.

Her house number is [1] _____.

The bus number is [2] _____.

Her telephone number is [3] _____.

Review

1 🔊 1.15 **Work in groups. Play the first letter game.**
- Listen to the letter of the alphabet.
- How many examples can you find for each category in the table?
- You get one point for each correct answer. The winner is the group with the most points.

	0 _p_	1 ___	2 ___	3 ___	4 ___	5 ___
Colour	pink purple					
Actor	Penelope Cruz Peter Jackson					
Classroom object	pen pencil					
Number (0–20)	—					
International word	pizza phone					
Total Points	8					

2 **Complete the words with the missing vowels and then write them in the correct column in the table below.**

0 f _o_ _o_ tb _a_ ll
1 d _ _ _ r
2 r _ st _ _ r _ nt
3 _ r _ ng _
4 p _ n
5 n _ n _

6 ch _ _ _ r
7 f _ v _
8 y _ ll _ w
9 _ _ rp _ rt
10 gr _ _ n
11 _ _ ght

International words	Colours	Numbers	Classroom objects
football			

3 SPEAKING **Work in pairs. Choose three pictures and spell the words for your partner to write. Is he/she correct?**

4 **Put the dialogues in order. Write 1–3 and 1–4 in the boxes.**

1

	JIM	Great, thanks. And you?
1	JIM	Good morning, Fred.
	FRED	I'm fine, thanks.
	FRED	Hi, Jim. How are you?

2

	LUCY	Yeah, have a good day.
	LUCY	Bye, Sara.
	SARA	Bye, Lucy. See you later.

1 | ONE WORLD

OBJECTIVES

FUNCTIONS: getting to know someone; talking about yourself and others

GRAMMAR: question words; the verb *to be*

VOCABULARY: countries and nationalities; adjectives

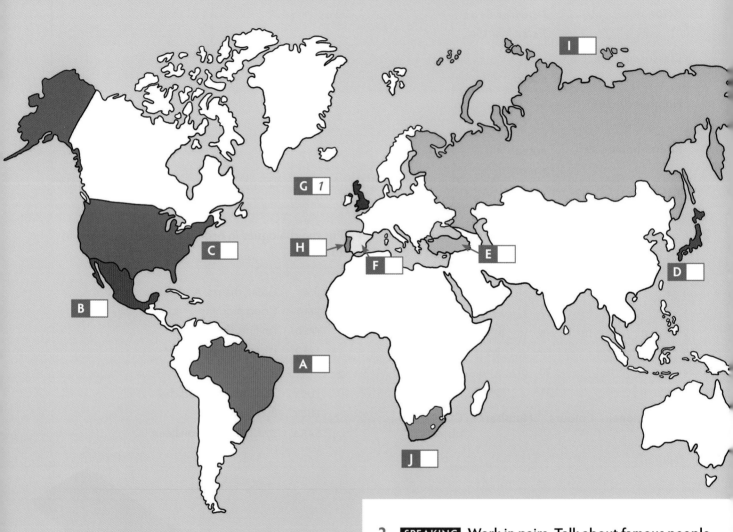

2 **SPEAKING** Work in pairs. Talk about famous people from different countries.

Neymar is from Brazil.

READING

1 **Match the names of the countries with the places on the map. Write 1–10 in the boxes.**

1	the UK	6	Brazil
2	Mexico	7	Portugal
3	the USA	8	Japan
4	Spain	9	Turkey
5	Russia	10	South Africa

3 **1.16** **Read and listen to the website and choose the correct words.**

0 Pedro is from *Brazil* / *the USA*.

1 Pedro is *10* / *11*.

2 Brittany is from *London* / *Manchester*.

3 Missy Franklin is a *swimmer* / *runner*.

4 Oleg is *Portuguese* / *Russian*.

5 Oleg is *11* / *12*.

6 Haruka is from *Japan* / *the UK*.

7 Zheng Jie is a *runner* / *tennis player*.

Mad about the Olympics

HOME ABOUT NEWS CONTACT

Tell us about your Olympic favourites!

What's your name?
Pedro.

Where are you from?
I'm Brazilian. I'm from a city called Belo Horizonte.

How old are you?
I'm 10.

Who's your favourite athlete?
Usain Bolt.

Why is he/she your favourite athlete?
Because he's amazing!

What's your name?
My name is Brittany.

Where are you from?
I'm British. I'm from Manchester.

How old are you?
I'm 12.

Who's your favourite athlete?
My favourite athlete is Missy Franklin. She's a swimmer.

Why is he/she your favourite athlete?
Because she's great!

What's your name?
I'm Oleg.

Where are you from?
I'm from Russia. I live in Moscow.

How old are you?
I'm 11.

Who's your favourite athlete?
Mariya Savinova. She's a runner.

Why is he/she your favourite athlete?
Because she's fast!

What's your name?
My name is Haruka.

Where are you from?
I'm Japanese. I'm from Tokyo.

How old are you?
I'm 11.

Who's your favourite athlete?
Zheng Jie. She's a tennis player from China.

Why is he/she your favourite athlete?
Because she's awesome!

■ THiNK VALUES ■
The Olympic Spirit
Choose a slogan for the website.
- [ ] One world together.
- [ ] Exercise is fun.
- [ ] Win, win, win!

VOCABULARY
Countries and nationalities

1 🔊 1.17 **Write the country under the flag. Listen and check.**

Brazil | Japan | Mexico | Portugal | ~~Russia~~
South Africa | Spain | the UK | the USA | Turkey

0 _____Russia_____

1 _____

2 _____

3 _____

4 _____

5 _____

6 _____

7 _____

8 _____

9 _____

2 **Look at Exercise 1. Complete the table with the nationalities of the countries.**

-an	-ish	-ese
	Spanish	

3 **SPEAKING** **Work in pairs. Describe a flag to your partner. He/She guesses which it is.**

> This flag is red and blue.

> Is it the Russian flag?

> Yes, it is!

Workbook page 13

GRAMMAR
Question words

1 **Look at the website on page 13 and complete the questions with the words in the list. Then choose the correct words to complete the rule.**

How | ~~What~~ | Where | Who | Why

0 _____What_____ 's your name?
1 _____ are you from?
2 _____ old are you?
3 _____ 's your favourite athlete?
4 _____ is he/she your favourite athlete?

> **RULE:** *How*, *Who*, *Where*, *What* and *Why* are
> [1]*question / because* words.
> We often use the word [2]*question / because* to
> answer a ***Why*** question.

2 **Choose the correct words.**

0 (*How*)/ *Why* old is your best friend?
1 *What / Where* is your mother from?
2 *How's / What's* your favourite colour?
3 *Where / Who* is your favourite pop star?
4 *Why / Where* is he/she your favourite pop star?

3 **SPEAKING** **Work in pairs. Ask and answer the questions in Exercises 1 and 2.**

> What's your name?

> My name is Belena.

Workbook page 10

Pronunciation
/h/ or /w/ in question words
Go to page 120.

LISTENING

1 Work in pairs. Look at the photos and tick (✓) the correct flag for each photo.

2 🔊 1.20 Listen to a radio quiz called *One-Minute Challenge* and check your answers.

GRAMMAR
to be

1 Match sentences a–h with items 1–4. Write the letters in the boxes.

1 Bruno Mars | e | ☐
2 Maria Sharapova | ☐ | ☐
3 sushi | ☐ | ☐
4 cariocas | ☐ | ☐

a She's Russian.
b It's Japanese.
c They are Brazilian.
d It's food.
e He's a singer.
f They are from Rio de Janeiro.
g She's a tennis player.
h He's American.

2 Look at the sentences from the radio quiz. Choose the correct words. Then complete the rule.

1 I *am* / *are* from London.
2 You *am* / *are* wrong.
3 They *am* / *are* from Rio de Janeiro in Brazil.

> **RULE:** The verb *to be* changes for different subject pronouns.
> *I **am** American.*
> *You/We/They* ¹_____ *American.*
> *He/She/It* ²_____ *American.*
> We often use contracted forms after pronouns.
> I am = I'm
> You/We/They are = You're / We're / They're
> He/She/It is = He's / She's / It's

> **LOOK!**
>
> | Singular | Plural |
> |----------|--------|
> | I | we |
> | you | you |
> | he/she/it | they |

3 Complete the sentences. Use contracted forms where possible.

0 I ′*m*_____ from New York.
1 She _____ a famous actor.
2 Jacob _____ from the USA.
3 Liam and Ben _____ my best friends.
4 We _____ in Class 2B.
5 You _____ wrong. Sorry.

Workbook page 11 ➡

▮ THiNK SELF-ESTEEM ▮

The 'Me' flag

1 Choose things that are important to you.

● one colour   ● two activities
● one animal

2 **SPEAKING** Use your ideas from Exercise 1 to draw your flag. Tell your partner about it.

My flag is blue and red. They're my favourite colours. Here is a football. It's my favourite sport. Here is music. I love music. Here is a panda. It's my favourite animal.

READING

1 🔊 1.21 **Read and listen to the dialogue. Who knows more about football, Jamie or Marta?**

JAMIE	Nice shirt.
MARTA	Thank you. It's the new Barcelona shirt.
JAMIE	I know. I'm a Barcelona fan, too. So what's your name?
MARTA	Marta. And what's your name?
JAMIE	I'm Jamie.
MARTA	Nice to meet you, Jamie.
JAMIE	Nice to meet you, too. Where are you from, Marta?
MARTA	I'm from Spain. I'm from a small town called Teruel.
JAMIE	Spain is a beautiful country.
MARTA	Yes, it is. So who's your favourite Barcelona player?
JAMIE	Umm … er … Tony Kroos?
MARTA	The German player?
JAMIE	Yes, he's great.
MARTA	Yes, he is. But he isn't a Barcelona player.
JAMIE	No?
MARTA	He's a Real Madrid player.
JAMIE	Oh!
MARTA	It's late. Time to go. Bye, Jamie.
JAMIE	Oh, OK!

2 **Read the dialogue again. Mark the sentences T (true) or F (false). Write the correct sentences.**

0 Jamie is a Real Madrid fan.   *F*
Jamie is a Barcelona fan.
1 Marta is Spanish.
2 Marta is from a big town.
3 Tony Kroos is Italian.
4 Tony Kroos is a Barcelona player.

3 **Write the questions.**

1 Q _____
A   I'm Jamie.
2 Q _____
A   I'm from a small town called Teruel.
3 Q _____
A   Tony Kroos.

FUNCTIONS
Getting to know someone

1 🔊 1.22 **Put the dialogue in order. Listen and check.**

☐	GINA	Nice to meet you, too.
☐	GINA	I'm from Paris.
☐	GINA	Yes, it is.
☐	GINA	I'm Gina.
1	GINA	What's your name?
☐	PAOLO	Nice to meet you, Gina.
☐	PAOLO	Where are you from, Gina?
☐	PAOLO	Paris is a beautiful city.
☐	PAOLO	I'm Paolo. And you?

2 **SPEAKING** **Work in pairs. Act out the dialogue.**

3 **SPEAKING** **Work in pairs. Make your own dialogue.**

VOCABULARY
Adjectives

1 🔊 1.23 **Write the words in the list under the pictures. Listen and check.**

~~a big TV~~ | a dirty football | a fast car | a new pen
a slow bus | a small pizza | an expensive computer
an old phone | cheap tickets | clean shirts

0 _____*a big TV*_____

1 _____

4 _____

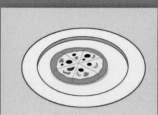

5 _____

2 _____

3 _____

8 _____

9 _____

6 _____

7 _____

2 Match the opposites.

0	new	*d*		a	slow
1	big			b	expensive
2	dirty			c	small
3	cheap			d	old
4	fast			e	clean

3 Put the words in order.

0 old / computer / an
   an old computer
1 a / bike / new
2 expensive / an / restaurant
3 train / fast / a
4 dirty / shoes
5 book / cheap / a

> **LOOK!** In English, adjectives always stay the same.
> *new pens* **NOT** ~~news pens~~
> *green cars* **NOT** ~~greens cars~~

Workbook page 13 ▸

WRITING
Personal information

Look at the questionnaire. Answer the questions about you in full sentences.

The York English
Summer Camp

We're really excited about your visit next month. Answer the questions about yourself to find the perfect roommate.

What's your name?

Where are you from?

How old are you?

Who's your favourite pop star?

What's your favourite colour?

Just a little joke

1 **Look at the photos and answer the questions.**

How many people can you see?
Where are they?

2 🔊 1.24 **Now read and listen to the photostory. Check your answers.**

RUBY Hi, Ellie.
ELLIE Hi, Ruby. How's it going?
RUBY Great, thanks. Oh, hello, Dan.
DAN Hi, you two.

1

RUBY Who's that?
DAN That's *Thomas*.
ELLIE Who's he?
DAN He's in my class. He's new.

2

ELLIE Where's he from?
DAN He's from Paris. He's cool. OK, time to go now. See you tomorrow.
RUBY Bye, Dan.
ELLIE See you later.

3

ELLIE He's from Paris?
RUBY Paris. That is so awesome!
ELLIE I know!

4

DEVELOPING SPEAKING

3 ◀ EP1 **Watch to find out how the story continues.**

1 Is Thomas from France?

2 Where is he from?

4 ◀ EP1 **Watch again. Choose the correct word in each sentence.**

0 They are in *an ice cream* / *a fast food* shop.

1 The chocolate ice cream is for *Ellie* / *Ruby*.

2 Thomas (Tom) is *American* / *French*.

3 He's from *Paris, Texas* / *Paris, France*.

4 The ice cream *is very good* / *isn't very good*.

PHRASES FOR FLUENCY

1 Find the expressions 1–4 in the story. Who says them?

1 How's it going?

2 See you later.

3 That is so awesome!

4 I know!

2 How do you say the expressions in Exercise 1 in your language?

3 Change the <u>underlined</u> expressions. Use an expression from Exercise 1.

1 A This is my new bicycle.

   B <u>Great</u>!

2 Hi, George. <u>How are you</u>?

3 A This is a nice computer.

   B <u>Yes, it is</u>.

4 OK, I'm off now. <u>Goodbye</u>!

4 Complete the dialogues with the expressions from Exercise 1.

0 A Moscow is a city in Russia.

   B *I know*   !

1 A Hello, Ben!

   B _____ ?

2 A Look at my new phone.

   B _____ !

3 A Goodbye, Mike.

   B _____ , Annie.

FUNCTIONS
Talking about yourself and others

1 Match the questions and answers.

0	Who's that?	b
1	Where's he from?	
2	How old are you?	
3	Who's your favourite singer?	

a He's from Paris.

b That's Thomas.

c Beyoncé.

d I'm 11.

2 Put the words in the correct order to make dialogues.

1 A that / who's ?

   Who's that?

   B Mary / that's .

   A she / from / where's ?

   B the UK / from / she's .

2 A they / are / who ?

   B Mario / are / and / they / Alex .

   A are / from / where / they ?

   B from / they / Mexico / are .

3 A Hi, / your / name / what's ?

   B Bob / I'm .

   A old / you, / how / are / Bob ?

   B 12 / I'm .

   A favourite / your / singer / who's ?

   B Ed Sheeran .

3 SPEAKING **Work in pairs. Act out the dialogues. Then make similar dialogues.**

2 I FEEL HAPPY

READING

1 Match the phrases with the photos. Write 1–6 in the boxes.

1 on a train	4 at school
2 on a plane	5 on a beach
3 at a stadium	6 on a bus

2 **SPEAKING** Work in pairs. Student A, close your book. Student B, test your partner.

What's A?

It's 'on a beach.'

3 🔊 1.25 **Read and listen to the text messages on page 21. Where are the people? Write the names under the correct photos in Exercise 1.**

4 Read the text messages again. Mark the sentences T (true) or F (false).

0	Nicky is worried.	T
1	Andrea is at school.	
2	Andrea, Amy and Katie are on holiday.	
3	Ryan is bored.	
4	The bus driver isn't angry.	
5	James isn't happy.	

A

B

C

D

E 1

F

Hi there!

Nicky

Hi there, I'm at school. There are 12 girls and 15 boys in my new class. They aren't very friendly. I'm a little worried. 😟 But the teacher's really cool. How are you? Are you OK? See you soon.

10.06

Andrea

Look at my photo. I'm on the beach. It's hot and sunny. I'm very happy. 😊 I'm with 2 American girls, Amy and Katie. It's fun! What about you? How's your holiday? Is it nice there?

3.26

Ryan

I'm on the bus to school and I'm not very happy. It's so full and I'm very hot. 😣 The driver isn't very nice and he's angry. Ten more minutes to get to school. See you soon!

8.16

James

Hi, I'm at the stadium. It's 4–0 to the other team. The players in my team aren't good. Are they tired or bored? I'm sad. 😞 Football is a great game, but this match isn't great. Bye.

4.58

■ THiNK VALUES ■

Welcoming a new classmate

1 **Look at the picture and answer the questions.**

1 Where is Emily?
2 How is she?
3 Why isn't Emily happy?

> The first day at my new school. I'm worried and I'm sad. Where are my friends?

2 **Imagine you are Emily's classmate. What's OK** 😊 **or not OK** 😟**?**

0 talk to Emily
1 help Emily   _____
2 smile at Emily   _____
3 laugh at Emily   _____
4 not talk to Emily   _____
5 ask Emily questions   _____

3 **SPEAKING Compare your ideas with a partner.**

> It's OK to smile at Emily.

> It isn't OK to ...

4 **SPEAKING Work in pairs. Think of other things you can do to help Emily on her first day.**

VOCABULARY
Adjectives to describe feelings

1 🔊 1.26 **Match the feelings in the list with the pictures. Write 1–10 in the boxes. Listen and check.**

1 angry | 2 bored | 3 cold | 4 excited
5 hot | 6 hungry | 7 sad | 8 thirsty
9 ~~tired~~ | 10 worried

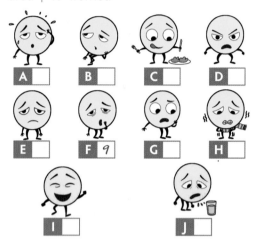

2 **Match the sentences with the pictures. Write 1–6 in the boxes.**

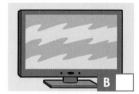

1 It's your birthday.
2 It's one o'clock in the morning.
3 There's a great film on TV but the TV is broken.
4 It's an awful day.
5 Your mum is angry with you.
6 You're on a plane.

3 SPEAKING **Work in pairs. Tell your partner how you feel in the situations in Exercise 2. Your partner guesses the situation.**

> I'm excited.

> Number 1?

Workbook page 21

GRAMMAR
to be (negative, singular and plural)

1 **Look at the text messages on page 21. Complete the sentences. Then complete the rule.**

1 They _____ very friendly.
2 The driver _____ very nice and he's angry.

> **RULE:** We form the negative of to be with subject + be + ¹_____ .
> I'm not sad. (am not)
> You aren't sad. (are not)
> He/She/It ²_____ sad. (is not)
> We aren't sad. (are not)
> They ³_____ sad. (are not)

2 **Complete the sentences with the correct negative form of to be.**

0 Adelaide ___isn't___ happy today. She's very sad.
1 You _____ in my team. You're in Mike's team.
2 They _____ eleven years old. They are ten.
3 No pizza for me, thanks. I _____ hungry.
4 Angie's favourite colour is blue. It _____ green.

3 **Complete the sentences with the correct form of to be.**

0 We ___'re___ ✓ American. We ___aren't___ ✗ British.
1 I _____ ✗ sad. I _____ ✓ happy!
2 Danny _____ ✓ twelve. He _____ ✗ eleven.
3 It _____ ✗ hot. It _____ ✓ cold!
4 Lucy _____ ✓ worried. She _____ ✗ excited.

Workbook page 18

Pronunciation
Vowel sounds – adjectives
Go to page 120.

▮TRAIN TO THiNK▮
Categorising

1 **Read the words in the list. Put them into four categories. There are four words for each category.**

afternoon | angry | book | bored | chair | desk
evening | excited | grey | morning | night
orange | pencil | purple | white | worried

2 SPEAKING **Work in pairs. Compare your categories. Think of a title for each one.**

> Category 1 - grey, orange, ...

LISTENING

1 **◀》1.29** Listen to four dialogues. Match two of the dialogues with the pictures. Write a number (1–4) in the boxes.

2 **◀》1.29** Listen again. Complete the dialogues with *cold*, *tired*, *excited* and *angry*.

0 A Is Noah's mum sad?
  B No, she isn't. She's _angry_ .

1 A Are Chris and David worried?
  B No, they aren't. They're _____ .

2 A Is Ted worried?
  B No, he isn't. He's _____ .

3 A Is Ashley hot?
  B No, she isn't. She's very _____ .

GRAMMAR

to be (questions and short answers)

1 Look at picture A in Exercise 1. Choose the correct answer. Then complete the rule and the table.

A Are you hot, Ashley?
B *Yes, I am. / No, I'm not.*

> **RULE:** We form questions with ¹_____ + subject.
> We form short answers with ²_____ + subject + *to be* (+ *not*).

Question	Short positive answer	Short negative answer
Am I in your team?	Yes, you **are**.	No, you **aren't**.
Are you OK?	Yes, I **am**.	No, I**'m** not.
¹_____ he/she/it OK?	Yes, he/she/it **is**.	No, ⁴_____ .
Are we in your team?	Yes, we are.	No, ⁵_____ .
²_____ they OK?	Yes, they ³_____ .	No, they **aren't**.

2 Put the words in order to make questions. Write the answers.

0 African / he / is / South / ? (yes)
  Is he South African? Yes, he is.
1 hungry / you / are / ? (no)
2 Brazil / they / from / are / ? (yes)
3 you / 12 / are / ? (yes)
4 she / is / tired / ? (no)
5 late / I / am / ? (no)

A

B

3 Look at the rule again. Complete the dialogues.

1 A _____ *Are* _____ you angry, Keira?
  B No, I _____ . I'm just tired.
2 A _____ James and Tim your best friends?
  B Yes, they _____ . They _____ in my class at school.
3 A _____ Ms Brown your English teacher?
  B No, she _____ . She's my mother's friend.
4 A Am I in your team?
  B No, you _____ . You're in Pam's team.
5 A _____ Jules French?
  B _____ . He's from Paris.
6 A _____ we late?
  B _____ . We're early.

4 **SPEAKING** Work in pairs. Ask and answer.

> *Is football your favourite sport?*

> *Are you cold?*

> *Are your best friends from the USA?*

> *Is your teacher in the classroom?*

5 **SPEAKING** Think of three more questions to ask your partner. Then ask and answer.

> Workbook page 18

READING

1 **◀)) 1.30** Read and listen to the dialogue and choose the correct option.

Nick and Connor decide to …

a   go to the cinema.

b   listen to music.

c   go to a club for young people.

2 Read the dialogue again. Number the photos in the order that Connor talks about them. Write 1–5 in the boxes.

CONNOR	What's the matter, Nick? Are you tired?
NICK	Tired? No, no. I'm not tired. I'm bored.
CONNOR	Why are you bored?
NICK	Because there's nothing to do. Nothing to do at all.
CONNOR	Well, there's a Formula One race at five. It's on TV.
NICK	Formula One? I don't like it.
CONNOR	Really? What about a film? There's a new film on at the cinema.
NICK	A film? Who's in it?
CONNOR	Ben Stiller. He's so funny.
NICK	Ben Stiller? I don't like him. He's not funny. He's terrible.
CONNOR	Erm. What about some music? Listen to this song. It's the new one from One Direction.
NICK	One Direction! Are you joking? I don't like them.
CONNOR	Well do you like ice cream? The new ice cream shop in town is open.
NICK	Ice cream? No, I don't like it.
CONNOR	What! You don't like ice cream?
NICK	No, I don't.
CONNOR	OK, what about the club?
NICK	What club?
CONNOR	The new club for teenagers.
NICK	Hmm, I'm not sure.
CONNOR	But Jenny is a member.
NICK	Jenny?
CONNOR	Yes, Jenny Carter.
NICK	Jenny Carter?
CONNOR	Yes, she goes there every Friday.
NICK	Really? Let's go!

3 Correct the sentences.

0   Nick is tired.
He isn't tired. He's bored.

1   The Formula One race is at eight.

2   Johnny Depp is in the film.

3   The song is by The Feeling.

4   The new T-shirt shop in town is open.

5   Nick is a member of the club for teenagers.

A

B

C

D *1*

E

GRAMMAR
Object pronouns

1 Complete the dialogues with *them*, *it* and *him*. Read the dialogue on page 24 again and check. Then use the words to complete the table.

CONNOR   There's a Formula One race at five.
NICK   Formula One? I don't like [1]_____ .

CONNOR   Ben Stiller is so funny.
NICK   I don't like [2]_____ .

CONNOR   Listen to this song.
NICK   One Direction! I don't like [3]_____ .

Subject	Object
I	me
you	you
he	[1]_____
she	her
it	[2]_____
we	us
they	[3]_____

2 Complete the dialogues with the correct object pronouns.

0 A Dad's angry.
   B Yes, he isn't very happy with ___us___ , Tom.
1 A Do you like Maroon 5?
   B No, I don't like _____ .
2 A Do you like Jennifer Lopez?
   B Yes, I like _____ . She's great.
3 A Do you like _____ ?
   B Yes, I think you and Peter are great.
4 A Do you like _____ ?
   B Yes, I think Jack is funny.
5 A Do you like my new bike?
   B Yes, I like _____ .
6 A Bob, I really like _____ .
   B I really like you too, Alice.

Workbook page 19

VOCABULARY
Positive and negative adjectives

1 Look at the words in the list. Write N (negative) or P (positive) in the boxes.

awful [N] | bad [ ] | excellent [P] | exciting [ ]
funny [ ] | good [ ] | great [ ] | terrible [ ]

2 **SPEAKING** Work in pairs. Give one example for each of the following.

> *How To Train Your Dragon 2 is a funny film.*

a a funny film
b an excellent actor
c a bad film
d an exciting computer game
e a great sportsperson
f a terrible singer
g a great country
h a good book
i an awful actor

Workbook page 21

FUNCTIONS
Expressing likes and dislikes

1 Which of these sentences means 'is good'? Which means 'is bad'?

1 I don't like Taylor Swift.
2 I like Shakira.

2 Put the words in the correct order to make questions.

A you / like / The Rolling Stones / do / ?
B you / Katy Perry / like / do / ?

3 Match the answers to the questions in Exercise 2.

1 No, I don't like them. They're terrible. [ ]
2 Yes, I like her. She's great. [ ]

4 **SPEAKING** Work in pairs. Talk about the films, actors, bands or singers you really like / don't like.

> *Do you like Lorde?*

> *Yes, I like her. I think she's great.*

> *Do you like the Divergent films?*

> *No, I don't like them. They're terrible.*

Masks from around the world

1 This is a lion mask from China. In many countries in Asia, there are lion dances. There are always two people in a lion – the mask is on the head of one dancer. The lion dances are very beautiful. Tourists *love* them.

2 This mask is from North America. It's a mask from the First Nations people in Canada. The mask is for the medicine man.

3 The masks here are from Greece. They are 2,000 years old. They are masks for the actors in the Greek theatre.

4 Masks are an important part of the carnival in Venice, Italy. There are many different types of carnival masks. For example, the mask in this picture is called the Colombina. Carnival masks are often very beautiful and some are very expensive.

5 These are Halloween masks. Halloween is on 31st October. Children in many countries around the world, for example, the USA and the UK, wear Halloween masks. They go from house to house and say 'Trick or treat'. People give them sweets ('treats').

1 Look at the photos on page 26. Find these things.

masks | a lion
a mask from the First Nations people
one dancer | sweets | tourists

2 What feelings can you see in the masks?

> *Mask number 1 is happy.*

3 🔊 1.31 Read and listen to the article. Which countries are the masks from?

4 Read the article again. Mark the sentences T (true) or F (false).

0	The Lion dance is from Canada.	F
1	The North American mask is for a doctor.	
2	The Greek masks are 200 years old.	
3	Halloween is only a holiday in the USA and the UK.	
4	Colombina is a type of Italian mask.	

5 **SPEAKING** Which of the masks do you like? Which do you not like? Why? Tell your partner.

WRITING
Describing feelings and things

1 Read the text messages. Write the names under the photos.

2 Read the text messages again and answer the questions.

1 Where is Henry?
2 Is he happy?
3 Why? / Why not?
4 Where is Tom?
5 Is he happy?
6 Why? / Why not?

3 How do Tom and Henry …

1 start their text?
2 finish their text?

4 Imagine you want to write a text message to a friend. Think of answers to these questions.

1 Where are you?
2 Are you happy?
3 Why? / Why not?

5 Use your answers in Exercise 4 to write a text message (35–50 words) to a friend.

Tom

Hi, Sara. I'm at school. It's lunchtime and I'm really hungry. But I'm sad. The lunch at school today isn't good. I'm also cold. The sun isn't out. It's not a great day. What about you? Is your day good? Bye.

21/1, 13.12

Henry

Hi, Annie. I'm in the car with my family. I'm excited because I'm on holiday. Yeah! Two more hours to get to the beach! How are you? Are you OK? See you soon!

16/6, 10.03

A

B

THiNK EXAMS

READING AND WRITING
Part 3: Multiple-choice replies

1 Complete the five conversations. Choose the correct answer A, B or C.

0 What's your name?
   A I'm 11.
   (B) It's Kylie.
   C Yes, I am.

1 How old are you?
   A I'm Brazilian.
   B I'm 12.
   C It's John.

2 Are we late?
   A Yes, we are.
   B No, I'm not.
   C Yes, he is.

3 Do you like Beyoncé?
   A No, I like her.
   B Yes, I am.
   C Yes, I like her.

4 Where are you from?
   A I'm 13.
   B Yes, I am.
   C Mexico.

5 Is Tom your friend?
   A Yes, we are.
   B Yes, he is.
   C Yes, I am.

Part 2: Multiple-choice sentence completion

2 Read the sentences about Jim. Choose the best word (A, B or C) for each space.

0 Hi, my name _____ Jim.
   A am   (B) is   C are

1 It _____ my birthday today.
   A are   B am   C is

2 I _____ 12 years old.
   A am   B is   C are

3 I am _____ my school.
   A at   B on   C to

4 I like Ed Sheeran. He's a(n) _____ singer.
   A great   B awful   C terrible

5 I _____ like sport.
   A aren't   B don't   C isn't

VOCABULARY

1 Complete the sentences with the words in the list. There are two extra words.

awful | Brazil | clean | excited | expensive | hot
hungry | old | Russian | Spain | Spanish | thirsty

1 I want a sandwich. I'm _____ .
2 She's from Moscow. She's _____ .
3 Open the window, please. I'm _____ !
4 This pizza is _____ . I don't like it!
5 He's _____ . I think he's from Madrid.
6 I'm 12 and my big brother Jack is 23. He's _____ !
7 Are you _____ ? OK, here's a glass of water.
8 £175? Oh, it's very _____ .
9 Brasilia is a big city in _____ .
10 We're on the train to Paris! We're very _____ !

/10

GRAMMAR

2 Complete the sentences with the words in the list.

don't | her | How | it | Where | Why

1 Mike and Annie aren't here. _____ are they?
2 This is my new shirt. I really like _____ .
3 She's my friend. I like _____ a lot.
4 _____ old are you?
5 I _____ like hamburgers.
6 A _____ are you here?
  B Because it's a nice place.

3 Find and correct the mistake in each sentence.

1 I not like football.
2 What old is your brother?
3 Are them from Italy?
4 It aren't an expensive computer.
5 He's the new boy in the class. I like he.
6 What is your favourite singer?

/12

FUNCTIONAL LANGUAGE

4 Write the missing words.

1 A Who _____ she?
  B She's Maria. She's _____ Mexico.
2 A _____ are they from?
  B Spain. They _____ Spanish.
3 A _____ you like Taylor Swift?
  B Yes, I do. She _____ a great singer.
4 A I _____ like this film. It's awful!
  B Oh, really? I _____ it. It's funny!

/8

MY SCORE /30

| 22 – 30 |
| 10 – 21 |
| 0 – 9 |

3 | ME AND MY FAMILY

A ☐

B ☐

C ☐

D 1

READING

1 Match the family members with the photos. Write 1–4 in the boxes.

1 brother and sister
2 mother and son
3 father and daughter
4 husband and wife

2 **SPEAKING** Think of famous examples of the following. Tell your partner.

1 a husband and wife
2 a mother and daughter
3 a father and son
4 sisters
5 brothers

> Brad Pitt and Angelina Jolie are a famous husband and wife.

3 **SPEAKING** Look at the photos on page 31. Use words from Exercise 1 to talk about the people.

4 ◀)) 1.32 Read and listen to the article. Mark the sentences T (true) or F (false).

0	Kate Middleton is from England.	*T*
1	She's got three brothers and sisters.	
2	Kate's picture is never in the newspapers.	
3	William's father is Prince Charles.	
4	Kate's home is new.	
5	Kate and William's apartment is small.	

Kate Middleton

William and Kate have a son called George and a daughter called Charlotte. George was born in 2013 and Charlotte was born in 2015.

Kate and William's home is an apartment in Kensington Palace, in London. The palace is 300 years old. Their apartment is really big, with twenty bedrooms and three kitchens.

Kate Middleton is an English woman. She likes sport (especially hockey) and photography. She's a very busy person. She works with many organisations to help children and sportspeople.

Kate's family is from Berkshire in England. She has a sister called Pippa and a brother called James.

So, is she a normal woman?

Not really. Now, she's famous all over the world. Her photograph is often in the newspapers and she's often on TV. She's The Duchess of Cambridge. Her husband is Prince William, the Duke of Cambridge. William's father is Prince Charles and his grandmother is Queen Elizabeth II of Britain.

■ THiNK VALUES ■

Families

1 **Complete the sentences with at least one word from the list. Use a dictionary to help you.**

friendly | interested in … | patient
helpful | kind | strict | generous

1 A good brother/sister is _____ .
2 A good father is _____ .
3 A good mother is _____ .
4 A good grandfather/grandmother is _____ .

2 **SPEAKING** **Compare your ideas with others in the class.**

GRAMMAR
Possessive 's

1 Look at the examples. Then complete the rule.

1 Kate's family is from Berkshire in England.
2 William's father is Prince Charles.

> **RULE:** We talk about possession with noun + 's.
> Peter _____ sister = the sister of Peter

2 Look at the photos and write the correct words with 's.

my sister

0 _____ *my sister's phone* _____

Patrick

1 _____

Mrs White

2 _____

my cousin

3 _____

Wendy

4 _____

my uncle

5 _____

> **LOOK!** We use **'s** for both possessives and contractions.
> Tom**'s** house is big. (~~The house of Tom is big.~~)
> She**'s** my cousin. (She is my cousin.)

Workbook page 28

VOCABULARY
Family members

1 🔊 **1.33 Complete Nicolás' family tree with the words in the list. Then listen and check.**

aunt | brother | cousin | father | grandfather
~~grandmother~~ | mother | sister | uncle

Maria   José
0 *grandmother*   1 _____

Pablo   Susana   Jaime   Marta
2 _____ 3 _____ 4 _____ 5 _____

Nicolás   Antonio   Ana   Sara
6 _____ 7 _____ 8 _____

2 Look at the text on page 31. Complete the sentences with the words in the list.

brother | ~~father~~ | grandfather | son | wife

0 William is George's ___ *father* ___.
1 Kate is William's _____ .
2 George is Kate's _____ .
3 Prince Charles is George's _____ .
4 James is Kate and Pippa's _____ .

3 SPEAKING Write three or four sentences about your family. Tell your partner.

> My uncle Antonio is my mother's brother.

Workbook page 31

GRAMMAR
Possessive adjectives

1 **Look at the article on page 31. Complete the sentences and match them with the people. Then complete the table.**

1 _____ grandmother is Queen Elizabeth. ☐

2 _____ husband is Prince William. ☐

3 _____ apartment is really big. ☐

a William and Kate

b William

c Kate

Subject	Possessive adjective
I	my
you	your
he	1 _____
she	2 _____
it	its
we	our
they	3 _____

2 **Complete the dialogue with words from Exercise 1.**

STEVE	Hello. ⁰ _My_ name's Steve. What's ¹_____ name?
JANE	Hi. I'm Jane and this is Renata. She's Brazilian. She's here on holiday with ²_____ mother and father.
STEVE	Hi, Renata.
RENATA	Hi, Steve. How are you?
STEVE	Fine, thanks. So, you and ³_____ parents are from Brazil?
RENATA	That's right – we speak Portuguese. It's ⁴_____ first language.
JANE	Have you got any brothers or sisters?
RENATA	No, just me! And you?
JANE	Yes, I've got two brothers. ⁵_____ names are Alex and Ricky. They love football! And they love Brazilian football!
RENATA	Great! My father is a football fan, too – ⁶_____ favourite team is Flamengo.

> Workbook page 28 ➤

LISTENING

1 🔊 1.34 **Listen to three people talking about their family. Write 1–3 in the boxes.**

A ☐

B ☐

C ☐

2 🔊 1.34 **Listen again and complete the sentences. Write one word in each space.**

1 Jordan's family is very _____ . His uncle Jack is always very _____ .

2 Tania's _____ are in Australia. Her _____ Clare is nice but sometimes she's difficult, too.

3 Manuel has _____ cousins. His cousin Monica is very _____ to her brothers, sisters and friends.

▌THiNK SELF-ESTEEM ▐
Being part of a family

1 **Complete the 'ME' table. Write the names of four people in your family who are important to you and a word to describe them.**

ME

	Name	Adjective
1		
2		
3		
4		

PARTNER

	Name	Adjective
1		
2		
3		
4		

2 **SPEAKING** Work in pairs. Ask your partner what he/she wrote. Write his/her answers in the 'PARTNER' table.

3 **SPEAKING** Tell the class about …

a your table.

b your partner's table.

READING

1 🔊 **1.35** **Read and listen to the dialogue and answer the questions.**

1 Where are the two girls?
2 Who is Brian?

2 **Read the dialogue again and answer the questions.**

1 Who's in the photograph?
2 Does Agata like her brother Brian?
3 Are the books and magazines Brian's?
4 Are the DVDs Agata's?
5 Does Brian like his sister?

AGATA	So, ⁰ _this_ is my bedroom. Do you like it?
DEBBIE	Yes! It's really nice. I like your bed. And the curtains are great!
AGATA	Thank you. I like my room, too. It's my favourite room in the house – of course!
DEBBIE	¹_____ is a nice photograph. There, on the desk.
AGATA	Yes, it's me and my family, on holiday in Ibiza. We're all very happy in that photograph!
DEBBIE	Cool. And is ²_____ your brother?
AGATA	Yes, it is. ³_____ is Brian.
DEBBIE	Oh, he's nice.
AGATA	Hmm … sometimes he is, sometimes he isn't.
BRIAN	Agata! Are you in here?
AGATA	Hi, Brian. Yes, I'm here. And ⁴_____ is my friend Debbie.
BRIAN	Hello, Debbie. Listen, Agata – are ⁵_____ your things?
AGATA	What things?
BRIAN	The books and magazines.
AGATA	Oh, yes, sorry.
BRIAN	And Agata, the DVDs on your bed – ⁶_____ are my DVDs!
AGATA	Yes, you're right. Sorry again.
BRIAN	You know something, Debbie? Sometimes my sister isn't my favourite person!

3 🔊 **1.35** **Complete the dialogue with the words in the list. Listen and check.**

this (x̶2̶) | that (x3) | these | those

GRAMMAR
this / that / these / those

1 **Match the sentences with the pictures. Write 1–4 in the boxes. Then choose the correct words to complete the rule.**

A

B 1

C

D

1 This is my sister.
2 That's my brother.
3 These are my pens.
4 Those are my friends.

> **RULE:** The words **this** and **that** are ¹*singular / plural*.
> The words **these** and **those** are ²*singular / plural*.
> We use **this** and **these** to talk about things that are ³*near to / far from* us.
> We use **that** and **those** to talk about things that are ⁴*near to / far from* us.

2 **Look at the pictures in Exercise 1 again. Complete the sentences with *this, that, these* or *those*.**

0 Picture A: Is ___*this*___ your phone?
1 Picture B: Are _____ your books?
2 Picture C: Are _____ your books?
3 Picture D: Is _____ your phone?

Workbook page 29

Pronunciation
this / that / these / those
Go to page 120. 🔊

VOCABULARY
House and furniture

1 🔊 1.38 **Match the rooms in the picture with the words. Write 1–7 in the boxes. Listen and check.**

bathroom	☐
bedroom	☐
garage	1
garden	☐
hall	☐
kitchen	☐
living room	☐

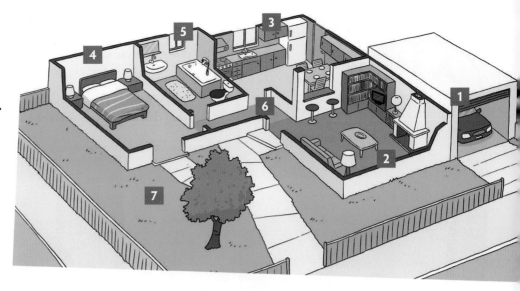

2 🔊 1.39 **Match the words with the photos. Write 1–8 in the boxes. Listen and check.**

1 armchair | **2** bath | **3** bed | **4** cooker | **5** fridge | **6** shower | **7** sofa | **8** toilet

A ☐   B ☐   C ☐   D ☐

E ☐   F ☐   G *1*   H ☐

3 Complete the table with words A–H from Exercise 2.

Living room	Kitchen	Bedroom	Bathroom

4 **SPEAKING** Draw an unusual house. Put the furniture in different rooms. Tell your partner about your house.

> *The fridge is in the living room.*
> *The toilet is in the kitchen.*

Workbook page 31

WRITING
Your favourite room

1 Think about your favourite room in your house. Answer the questions.

- Which room is it?
- Is it big or small?
- What things are in the room?
- What colours are the things in the room?

2 Write a description of your favourite room (about 50 words).

A song for Ruby

1 Look at the photos and answer the questions.

Where are the four friends?
How does Tom feel in photo 4?

2 🔊 1.40 Now read and listen to the photostory. What song does Tom's dad want to play?

TOM Come in, guys.
RUBY Wow, this photo is cool!
TOM Thank you.
DAN What's that photo over there?

1

TOM That's my family. We're on holiday.
RUBY It looks great. So, these are your parents and ...
ELLIE ... that's your sister?
TOM No, that's my cousin. My sister is there.
ELLIE Oh, right. She looks like your sister!

2

DAD Hello, everyone.
DAN Hello.
TOM Dad, these are my friends. This is Dan, and that's Ellie, and this is Ruby.

3

DAD Ruby? Really?
RUBY Yes. Why?
DAD Well, there's a great song called *Ruby*. Just a minute. Where's my guitar?
TOM OK, guys, let's go. I want to show you my room.

4

DEVELOPING SPEAKING

3 ▶️ **EP2** **Watch to find out how the story continues.**

1 What things do Tom's friends like about the house?
2 Do they like Tom's dad?

4 ▶️ **EP2** **Watch again. Match the parts of the sentences.**

0	Tom isn't very happy	*f*
1	Tom isn't a big fan of car racing,	
2	The armchair in Tom's room	
3	The garden in Tom's house	
4	They listen to music	
5	Ruby says Tom's dad	

a is broken.
b is really cool.
c in the living room.
d but he likes the poster of a racing car.
e isn't very big.
f about his dad.

PHRASES FOR FLUENCY

1 Find the expressions 1–4 in the story. Who says them?

1 Let's go.
2 Oh, right.
3 Really?
4 Just a minute.

2 How do you say the expressions in Exercise 1 in your language?

3 Put the sentences in the correct order to make a dialogue.

	TOM	Just a minute. Let me look at the map.
	TOM	Thanks. Oh. Sorry, Sally, this is the wrong map.
	TOM	Thanks. Ah, we're on the right road. Let's go.
1	SALLY	Where are we?
	SALLY	Really? Oh, right. Sorry. Here's the right map.
	SALLY	OK. The map's here. Here you are.

4 Complete the dialogues with the expressions from Exercise 1.

1 A I love this band. They're fantastic.
  B _____ ? I don't like them.
2 A This is a photo of my best friend.
  B _____ . She's very nice.
3 A Are you ready?
  B _____ , where's my phone?
  Oh, here it is. _____ .

FUNCTIONS
Paying compliments

1 Read the phrases. Tick (✓) five compliments.

1	This photo looks cool.	✓
2	Thank you.	
3	That's nice!	
4	That's my family.	
5	That's great.	
6	What a nice (picture)!	
7	I really like (your music).	

2 Tick the situations when you pay a compliment.

1	Your friend has got a new shirt.	
2	It's a sunny day.	
3	Your friend's sister is in New York on holiday.	
4	There is a great poster on your friend's bedroom wall.	
5	It's your friend's birthday.	
6	You like your friend's cat.	

3 Put the sentences in the correct order to make dialogues.

1	*1*	A	This photo is great.
		A	Is that your sister in the photo? She looks nice.
		B	Yes, her name's Carol. She's 14.
		B	Thanks. I like it, too.

2		A	Where's it from?
		A	I really like your shirt.
		B	Oh, thank you.
		B	It's from my holiday in Brazil.

4 **SPEAKING** **Act out the dialogues. Then change them and make similar dialogues.**

4 IN THE CITY

READING

1 Match the phrases in the list with the photos. Write 1–4 in the boxes.

1 a famous square | 2 a famous tower
3 a famous palace | 4 a famous statue

2 **SPEAKING** Work in pairs. Can you name the places in the photographs? Where are they?

> *I think it's the Eiffel Tower. It's in Paris.*

3 **1.41** Read and listen to the brochure. Which two things in Exercise 1 are in *Window of the World*?

4 Read the brochure again. Mark the sentences T (true) or F (false).

0 *Window of the World* is in China. `T`

1 All the models are of things in the same country.

2 There are models of 130 different things.

3 You can ski at *Window of the World*.

4 There is a train station in the park.

5 There are restaurants at *Window of the World*.

5 **SPEAKING** Work in pairs. Ask and answer the questions.

1 Would you like to go to *Window of the World*?

2 What would you like to see there?

A

B

C

D 1

Window of the World

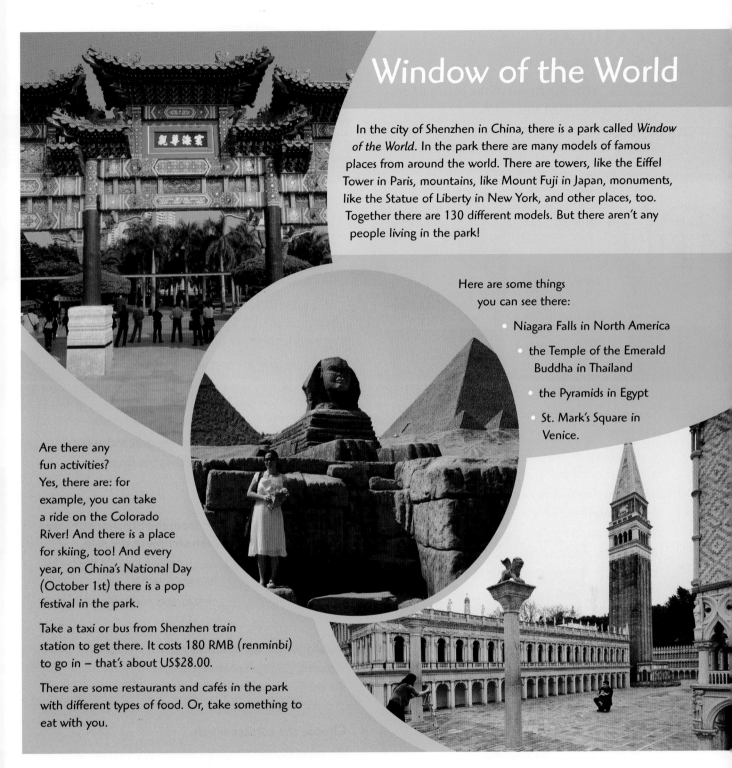

In the city of Shenzhen in China, there is a park called *Window of the World*. In the park there are many models of famous places from around the world. There are towers, like the Eiffel Tower in Paris, mountains, like Mount Fuji in Japan, monuments, like the Statue of Liberty in New York, and other places, too. Together there are 130 different models. But there aren't any people living in the park!

Here are some things you can see there:

- Niagara Falls in North America
- the Temple of the Emerald Buddha in Thailand
- the Pyramids in Egypt
- St. Mark's Square in Venice.

Are there any fun activities? Yes, there are: for example, you can take a ride on the Colorado River! And there is a place for skiing, too! And every year, on China's National Day (October 1st) there is a pop festival in the park.

Take a taxi or bus from Shenzhen train station to get there. It costs 180 RMB (renminbi) to go in – that's about US$28.00.

There are some restaurants and cafés in the park with different types of food. Or, take something to eat with you.

▮ THiNK VALUES ▮

My town/city

1 **Think of your town/city and answer the questions.**

  1 What are the most interesting places for you?
  2 What are the most interesting places for a visitor?

2 **SPEAKING Make one list of interesting places for you and one for a visitor. Tell your partner.**

  The most interesting places in my town/city for me are ...

  The most interesting places in my town/city for a visitor are ...

3 **Think of a place in your town, city or country to put in *Window of the World*.**

  1 What's the name of the place?
  2 Why do you want it in *Window of the World*?

  I want to put ... from my city because it's very old and beautiful.

4 **SPEAKING Compare your ideas with others in the class.**

VOCABULARY
Places in a town/city

1 ▶)) 1.42 **Write the names of the places under the pictures. Listen and check.**

bank | chemist's | library | museum | ~~park~~
post office | restaurant | supermarket | train station

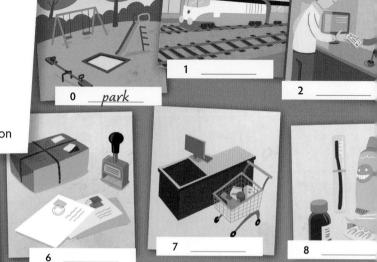

0 _park_
1 _____
2 _____

3 _____
4 _____
5 _____
6 _____
7 _____
8 _____

2 **Complete each sentence with a place from Exercise 1.**

0 You buy milk in a _supermarket_ .
1 You play football in a _____ .
2 You eat lunch or dinner in a _____ .
3 You send letters in a _____ .
4 You get on a train in a _____ .
5 You buy medicine in a _____ .
6 You look at interesting things in a _____ .
7 You read books in a _____ .

> Workbook page 39

GRAMMAR
there is / there are

1 **Complete the sentences from the brochure on page 39. Use *is*, *are* and *aren't*. Then complete the table.**

1 In the city of Shenzhen in China, there _____ a park called *Window of the World*.
2 _____ there any fun activities?
3 But there _____ any people living in the park!

	Singular nouns	Plural nouns
Positive	There ¹_____	There ³_____
Negative	There isn't	There ⁴_____
Questions	²_____ there?	⁵_____ there?

2 **Complete the sentences in the positive (+), negative (-) or question (?) form. Use *there is*, *there are*, *is there*, *there aren't* and *are there*.**

0 _There are_ six bridges in the city. (+)
1 _____ any good films on TV tonight. (-)
2 _____ a museum in your town?
3 _____ a great café near here. (+)
4 _____ any people in the park today. (-)
5 _____ any nice shops in this street?

some / any

3 **Complete the sentences from the brochure on page 39 with *some* or *any*. Then complete the rule.**

1 But there aren't _____ people living in the park!
2 Are there _____ fun activities?
3 There are _____ restaurants and cafés in the park.

> **RULE:** We use *some* and *any* with plural nouns.
> We use ¹_____ in positive sentences.
> We use ²_____ in negative sentences and questions.

4 **Choose the correct words.**

0 There are (some)/ any interesting things in the museum.
1 There aren't *some / any* parks in my town.
2 Are there *some / any* good shops here?
3 There are *some / any* nice places to eat here.

5 **SPEAKING Work in pairs. Think of a city, but don't tell your partner! Ask and answer questions to find out the cities.**

Is there a famous park in your city? | Yes, there is.

Is there a famous statue? | Yes, there is.

Is it New York?

> Workbook page 36

VOCABULARY
Prepositions of place

1 **Look at the map and complete the sentences with the words in the list.**

behind | between | in front of | next to
~~on the corner (of)~~ | opposite

1 A is *on the corner (of)* Green Street and High Street and _____ the supermarket.
2 B is _____ the library.
3 C is _____ the bank.
4 D is _____ the park and the post office.
5 E is _____ the restaurant.

Workbook page 39

LISTENING

1 ◀)) 1.43 **Listen to three people asking for directions. Write *museum*, *chemist's* and *shopping centre* in the correct places on the map. There are two extra spaces.**

2 ◀)) 1.43 **Listen again and complete the sentences.**

0 The chemist's is _____*opposite*_____ the library.
1 The chemist's is _____ the bank.
2 The museum is on _____ Green Street.
3 The shopping centre is _____ a restaurant.

GRAMMAR
Imperatives

1 **Complete the examples with *don't*, *turn* and *go*. Then complete the rule.**

1 _____ past the supermarket.
2 _____ left.
3 _____ take a bus – it's only two minutes from here.

> **RULE:** To tell someone to do something, you can use the **imperative** – it's the same as the base form of the verb.
>
> To tell someone **not** to do something, use [1]_____ + the base form of the verb.

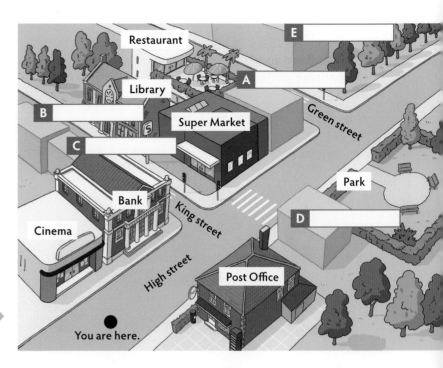

2 **Match the parts of the sentences.**

0	Listen	*b*
1	Sit	
2	Don't open	
3	Don't look	
4	Turn	
5	Go	

a the door.
b to me.
c right.
d down, please.
e down the street.
f at the answers.

Workbook page 37

FUNCTIONS
Giving directions

1 **SPEAKING Work in pairs. Look at the map again. Student A: You're at the restaurant. Student B: Think of another place on the map, but don't say it! Tell Student A how to find you.**

> *OK, turn right and right again into High Street. Turn right into King Street. It's on the right.*

> *The supermarket?*

> *That's right!*

2 **SPEAKING Now change. Student B: You're in the park. Student A: Choose another place on the map and tell Student B how to get there.**

READING

1 🔊 1.44 **Read and listen to the dialogues. Where are the people? Write a letter in each box. There are two extra letters.**

A bookshop | **B** chemist's | **C** shoe shop
D supermarket | **E** train station

1 ☐

MAN	Morning. Can I ⁰ _help you_ ?
GIRL	Yes, please. A ticket to London, please.
MAN	Return?
GIRL	Yes, please – a day return. ¹ _____ is it?
MAN	Well, it's £27.50 – but you can't come back between four o'clock and seven o'clock.
GIRL	Oh, no problem. Here you are – thirty pounds.
MAN	Thank you. And … two pounds fifty change.
GIRL	Thanks a lot.
MAN	OK. Oh! Don't forget your tickets!
GIRL	Oh, yes – thanks. Silly me.

2 ☐

WOMAN	These are nice. I really like them.
MAN	Yes, they're really nice.
WOMAN	And they're very comfortable. How much ² _____ ?
MAN	They're £120.
WOMAN	Wow. They're expensive.
MAN	Yes, but they're beautiful shoes.
WOMAN	You're right. OK, I'll ³ _____ them.
MAN	Great!

3 ☐

WOMAN	Hello.
GIRL	Hi. ⁴ _____ take these, please?
WOMAN	OK. Wow, that's a lot of books.
GIRL	That's right. There are twelve. Well, I'm a student.
WOMAN	Oh, right! So, here we go. Right – that's £135, please.
GIRL	OK. Here's my credit card.
WOMAN	Thank you. OK, bye – have ⁵ _____ .
GIRL	You too. Thank you!

2 **Complete the dialogues with the words and phrases in the list.**

a nice day | are they | Can I
~~help you~~ | How much | take

3 **SPEAKING** **Work in pairs. Act out the dialogues.**

VOCABULARY
Numbers 100+

1 🔊 1.45 **Match the words with the numbers. Then listen, check and repeat.**

0	130	*d*
1	150	☐
2	175	☐
3	200	☐
4	560	☐
5	1,000	☐
6	1,200	☐
7	2,000	☐

a five hundred and sixty
b one thousand two hundred
c two hundred
d one hundred and thirty
e one hundred and seventy-five
f one thousand
g two thousand
h one hundred and fifty

> **LOOK!** When a number is more than 100, we use the word ***and***:
> *one hundred **and** twenty*
> *two hundred **and** sixty-five*
> We **don't** use the word *and* for numbers 20–99.
> *twenty-five* **NOT** ~~*twenty and five*~~
> *seventy-three* **NOT** ~~*seventy and three*~~

2 🔊 1.46 **Listen and write the numbers.**

Workbook page 39

Pronunciation
Word stress in numbers
Go to page 120.

VOCABULARY
Prices

1 🔊 1.49 Say these prices. Listen and check.

1. £15.00
2. $25.00
3. €230.00
4. £9.99
5. $21.95
6. €72.50

> **LOOK!** $ = dollar(s)   £ = pound(s)   € = euro(s)
>
> £2.50 – In everyday English, we say *two pounds fifty* **not** *two pounds and fifty pence*.

2 🔊 1.50 Listen and look at the prices. Number them in the order you hear them.

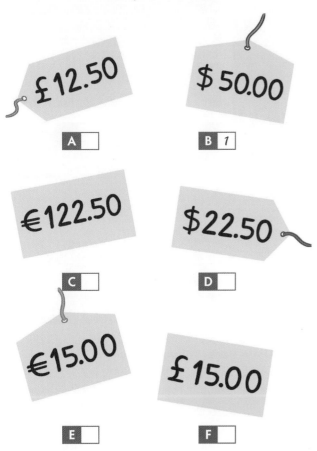

A ☐   B ☐ 1

C ☐   D ☐

E ☐   F ☐

3 **SPEAKING** Work in pairs. Ask and answer the questions. Student A: Go to page 127. Student B: Go to page 128.

Workbook page 39 ➤

FUNCTIONS
Buying in a shop

1 Read these questions and answers. Who says them? Write C (customer) or A (shop assistant).

1. Can I help you?   A
2. I'll take them.   ☐
3. How much are they?   ☐
4. Here's your change.   ☐
5. That's £ … , please.   ☐
6. Have you got … ?   ☐

2 Use the questions and answers from Exercise 1 to complete the dialogue. Write 1–6.

A Hi there. ___1___
B Hello. Yes, please. _____ any music magazines?
A Sure. There's this one here and there's also this one.
B Great. _____
A This one is £3.95 and the other one is £3.50.
B OK – _____
A Great. _____ £7.45, _____
B OK, Here you are. £10.00.
A Thank you. _____ – £2.55.
B Thanks. Bye!

3 🔊 1.51 Listen and check. Then act out the dialogue with a partner.

▮ TRAIN TO THiNK ▮
Exploring numbers

1 Read, think and write the answers.

Susan, Ian and George go shopping. Susan has got £20. Ian has got £12 and George has got £2. Susan spends £1.40 at the book shop and £3.30 at the supermarket and £8.30 at the café. Ian spends £3.80 at the post office and £2.20 at the chemist's.

At home, Mum says, 'How much money have you got now?'

Susan: £_____
Ian: £_____
George: £_____

2 Then Mum says: 'OK, Ian and Susan. Give George some money so that you all have the same!'

Susan gives George £_____ .
Ian gives George £_____ .

Culture

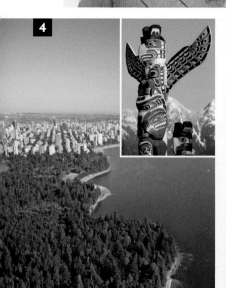

Parks
around the world

A ☐ Hyde Park, London, England

There are many parks in London. Hyde Park is a very big one. Many tourists and Londoners go there every day. There are paths for people on bicycles and there are often music concerts in the park.

B ☐ Stanley Park, Vancouver, Canada

Vancouver is a city near the sea and mountains. There is beautiful Stanley Park in the city centre. Over eight million people go there every year. There are First Nations totem poles in the park.

C ☐ Park Güell, Barcelona, Spain

In this park, designed by Antoni Gaudí, there are different houses in different colours. There are also things like a colourful dragon. From the park you can see the city of Barcelona and the sea.

D ☐ Ueno Park, Tokyo, Japan

Ueno Park is an old park in the city of Tokyo and there are hundreds of beautiful cherry trees. In April and May every year, the trees are pink or white.

E ☐ The Iguana Park, Guayaquil, Ecuador

The real name of this small park is Parque Simon Bolivar, but everyone calls it The Iguana Park because it is full of iguanas. The iguanas are very friendly. People in the city go there and feed them.

F 1 Chapultepec Park, Mexico City, Mexico

This is the biggest city park in Latin America. It's a very important green space in this big city. It has a lake and many museums. People in Mexico City love going there.

1 Look at the photos on page 44. Find these five things and one action.

a dragon | a lake | cherry trees
mountains | sea | feed (verb)

2 🔊 1.52 Read and listen to the article. Match the photos with the texts. Write 1–6 in the boxes.

3 Read the article again. Which parks are these sentences about? Write A–F in the boxes.

0 It isn't a new park. ☐ D

1 There are museums inside the park. ☐

2 You can ride your bicycle in the park. ☐

3 It's possible to see the sea from the park. ☐

4 You can see animals in this park. ☐

5 It isn't the only park in that city. ☐

WRITING
A brochure for your town / city

1 Read Paul's brochure for his town, Alderley Edge. What four things does the town have for visitors?

2 <u>Underline</u> the adjectives that Paul uses to describe the good things in the town.

3 Write a brochure for your town/city. Remember to:

- write a sentence to introduce your town (name, where it is).
- say what there is in the town.
- give some ideas for things to do there.
- write a closing sentence.

4 Now write your brochure (35–50 words).

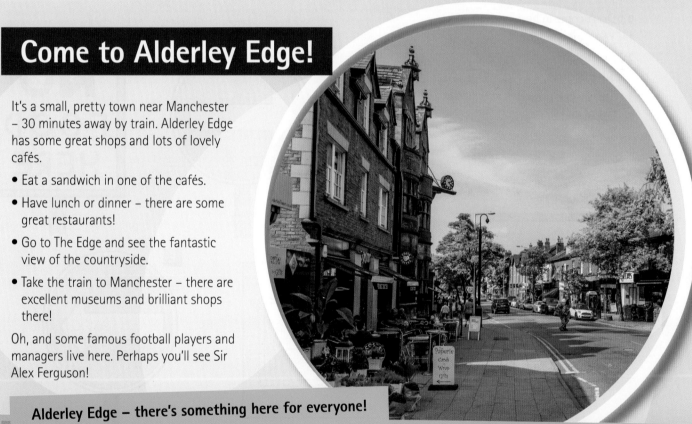

Come to Alderley Edge!

It's a small, pretty town near Manchester – 30 minutes away by train. Alderley Edge has some great shops and lots of lovely cafés.

- Eat a sandwich in one of the cafés.
- Have lunch or dinner – there are some great restaurants!
- Go to The Edge and see the fantastic view of the countryside.
- Take the train to Manchester – there are excellent museums and brilliant shops there!

Oh, and some famous football players and managers live here. Perhaps you'll see Sir Alex Ferguson!

Alderley Edge – there's something here for everyone!

READING AND WRITING
Part 6: Word completion

1 **Read the descriptions of some places in a town. What is the word for each one?**
The first letter is already there. There is one space for each other letter in the word.

0 You catch a train here. s _t a t i o n_

1 There are lots of old and interesting things here. m _ _ _ _ _ _

2 You put your money here. b _ _ _

3 Children play here. p _ _ _ _

4 You buy your food here. s _ _ _ _ _ _ _ _ _ _ _ _

5 You sit and eat here. r _ _ _ _ _ _ _ _ _ _

Part 1: Matching

2 **Which notice (A–H) says this (1–5)? Write the letters A–H in the boxes.**

0 Don't come in here.   G

1 You can send letters here.

2 Don't sit here.

3 Turn left.

4 The shop is not open at 5.30 pm.

5 Don't eat here.

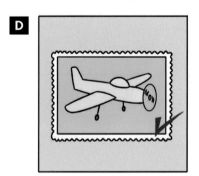

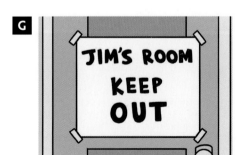

TEST YOURSELF

VOCABULARY

1 **Complete the sentences with the words in the list. There are two extra words.**

bathroom | cooker | garage | garden | grandfather | husband
kitchen | library | on the corner of | opposite | sofa | wife

1 Come and sit on the _____ . Let's watch TV.
2 There's a new fridge in the _____ . It's really big!
3 There's a _____ next to the fridge in the kitchen.
4 The cinema is _____ George Street and Smith Street.
5 There's a bath and a shower in our _____ .
6 She's Mr Graham's _____ . Her name's Pauline.
7 Our house is nice but there isn't a _____ for the car.
8 I love going to the _____ and reading books.
9 The supermarket is _____ the bank.
10 We really love our _____ . He's seventy-two years old now.

/10

GRAMMAR

2 **Complete the sentences with the words in the list.**

any | my | some | that | there | those

1 Is _____ a library here?
2 Hey! Is _____ your phone? Don't leave it on the desk.
3 How much are _____ black shoes, please?
4 There aren't _____ good films on TV tonight.
5 Are you hungry? Eat _____ sandwiches.
6 Please give me back _____ tablet.

3 **Find and correct the mistake in each sentence.**

1 There are a really big supermarket in town.
2 Do you like me new phone?
3 I don't like this shoes.
4 Doesn't open the window – it's cold in here!
5 That's bike's Jack.
6 Come and play at us house.

/12

FUNCTIONAL LANGUAGE

4 **Complete the missing words.**

1 A Hello. Can I h _ _ _ you?
  B Yes, please. H _ _ m _ _ _ _ are these shoes?
  A £32.99.
  B Great! I'll t _ _ _ them.
2 A Excuse me. W _ _ _ _ is the bank?
  B It's in Green Street. It's n _ _ _ _ to the supermarket.
  A In Green Street?
  B Yes, walk up here and t _ _ _ left. It's o _ _ _ _ _ _ _ _ _ a restaurant.

/8

MY SCORE /30

| 22 – 30 |
| 10 – 21 |
| 0 – 9 |

5 IN MY FREE TIME

OBJECTIVES

FUNCTIONS: talking about habits and activities; talking about technology habits; encouraging someone

GRAMMAR: present simple; adverbs of frequency; present simple (negative and questions)

VOCABULARY: free-time activities; gadgets

A

B 1

C

D

READING

1 Match the activities in the list with the photos. Write 1–4 in the boxes.

   1 listen to music | **2** play sport
   3 sing | **4** watch TV

2 Read the newsletter quickly. Which of the activities in Exercise 1 does it talk about?

3 ◁)) 1.53 **Read and listen to the newsletter. Mark the sentences T (true) or F (false).**

0 Miss Higgins is a Maths teacher.	*T*
1 The Glee club always sings new songs.	
2 The Glee club gives two concerts every year.	
3 Other students always like the Glee club concerts.	
4 The Glee club is only for Year Seven students.	
5 The Glee club meets two days a week.	

HOME | ABOUT | NEWS | CONTACT

Our school has a Glee club and it's brilliant. I know this because I'm a member! So what is a Glee club? Simple – it's a club for singing and I love singing.

Miss Higgins is the club leader. She chooses the songs and helps us to sing them. She plays the piano, too. She's really cool and she's really kind. She never gets angry with us. She's not even the school Music teacher. She teaches Maths, but she just loves singing.

We often sing popular songs from films but we sometimes sing old songs from the 1960s and 1970s. Three times a year we perform our songs in front of the rest of the school in a special concert. I feel so happy when I'm on stage. The teachers and the other students always cheer when we finish. It feels wonderful.

I love Glee club. Music is a great way to bring people together. You make so many friends at Glee club and not just with people from your school year. Glee club is for all ages.

We meet in the school hall every Tuesday at lunchtime and every Friday after school. Come and join us – we are always happy to see new people!

■ THiNK VALUES ■

Better together or better alone?

1   It's good to do some things on your own. But some things are better with friends. Look at the table and tick (✓) the answers for you.

	On my own	With friends
listen to music		
play sport		
play computer games		
watch TV		
do homework		

2   **SPEAKING** Tell your partner.

> *I listen to music on my own.*

GRAMMAR
Present simple

1 Look at the newsletter on page 49. Complete the sentences with the correct form of the verbs in the list. Then complete the rule.

cheer | ~~love~~ | make | meet | play

0 I _____love_____ Glee club!
1 You _____ so many friends at Glee club.
2 She _____ the piano, too.
3 We _____ in the school hall.
4 The teachers and other students always _____ when we finish.

> **RULE:** We add **-s** to the base form of the verb when the subject is *he*, [1]_____ or [2]_____ .
>
> **Spelling:** If the verb ends in *consonant + -y*, we change the *y* to an *i* and add *-es*.
> E.g. *study* → *stud**ies***
> If the verb ends in *-ch, -sh, -ss* or *-x*, we add *-es*.
> E.g. *watch* → *watch**es***

2 Write the correct third person form of the verbs in the list. Add *-s*, *-es* or *-ies*.

carry | choose | finish | fly | get | go
help | love | miss | study | teach | watch

> ### Pronunciation
> **Present simple verbs – third person**
> **Go to page 120.**

Adverbs of frequency

3 Look at the newsletter on page 49 and complete the sentences. Then complete the rule.

0 She _____never_____ gets angry with us.
1 We _____ sing popular songs.
2 We _____ sing old songs.
3 We're _____ happy to see new people.

> **RULE:**
> [1]_____ [2]_____ [3]_____ *always*
> 0% ————————→ 100%
> With the verb *to be* the adverb of frequency usually comes [4]*before / after* the verb.
> With other verbs, the adverb of frequency usually comes [5]*before / after* the verb.

Workbook page 46

VOCABULARY
Free-time activities

1 🔊 1.56 Match the activities in the list with the photos. Write 1–6 in the boxes. Listen and check.

1 chat to friends online | 2 dance
3 do homework | 4 go shopping
5 hang out with friends | 6 play computer games

 A

 B

 C

 D

 E

 F 1

2 Put the words in order to make sentences.

0 computer games / in the morning / I / play / never
I never play computer games in the morning.
1 often / with friends / hang out / in the park / we
2 sad / I / when / I'm / never / dance
3 goes / with her mum / she / sometimes / shopping
4 after school / always / his homework / does / he

3 Complete the sentences with an adverb of frequency so that they are true for you.

1 I _____ play computer games in the evening.
2 I _____ go shopping with my friends.
3 I _____ do my homework in the morning.
4 I _____ dance in my living room.
5 I _____ chat to my friends online after school.

4 **SPEAKING** Work in pairs. Compare your sentences from Exercise 3. Is anything the same? Compare your sentences with others in the class.

Workbook page 49

LISTENING

1 🔊 **1.57** **Listen and write the names under the photos.**

Harry | Julia | Shona | ~~Tim~~

A

B

Tim

C

D

2 🔊 **1.57** **Listen again and correct the adverb of frequency in each sentence.**

1 Tim sometimes uses the tablet to do his homework.
2 Shona doesn't often watch TV with her family.
3 Julia never plays _Minecraft_™ online with her friends.
4 Harry never uses his phone to text his friends.

3 **SPEAKING** **Work in pairs. Tell your partner what technology you use and what you use it for. Use adverbs of frequency.**

> _I sometimes use my computer for shopping._

GRAMMAR
Present simple (negative)

1 **Match the parts of the sentences. Then complete the rule.**

0	I use it to text my friends because	d
1	We don't watch TV together in our house;	
2	It's free;	
3	When Mum calls me for dinner,	

a it doesn't cost anything.
b we watch things on the computer.
c I don't want to stop playing.
d it doesn't cost a lot of money.

RULE: We use **don't** and **doesn't** [1] _before / after_ the verb to make negative sentences.

I/you/we/they + [2] _____ + base form
he/she/it + [3] _____ + base form
NOT _don't/doesn't_ + present simple form
e.g. ~~He doesn't likes music~~

2 **Make the sentences negative.**

0 I like Maths.
I don't like Maths.
1 The lesson finishes at two o'clock.
2 My brother helps me with my homework.
3 We go swimming on Sundays.
4 They watch a lot of TV.
5 My aunt lives in Quito.

3 **Complete the sentences with the correct form of the verbs in brackets.**

1 I sometimes ___play___ (play) computer games with my mum but I _____ (not play) them with my dad.
2 My brother _____ (not do) his homework after school. He _____ (do) it in the morning before school.
3 They often _____ (go) to clubs on Friday night but they _____ (not like) dancing.
4 Susie _____ (not hang out) with her friends after school. She _____ (go) home.
5 I always _____ (listen) to music in the kitchen but my dad _____ (not like) it.

> Workbook page 47

■ THiNK SELF-ESTEEM ■
What makes me happy?

1 **Tick (✓) what makes you happy.**

	Me	My partner
watch TV		
listen to music		
play computer games		
go shopping		
chat with friends online		
hang out with friends		

2 **SPEAKING** **Work in pairs. Tell each other two things that make you feel happy and two things that don't. Then tell the class about you and your partner.**

> _I'm happy when I watch TV._

> _Paolo isn't happy when he goes shopping._

Does TV control your life?

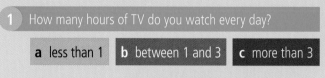

1 How many hours of TV do you watch every day?

a less than 1   **b** between 1 and 3   **c** more than 3

2 Do you watch TV before school?

a never   **b** sometimes   **c** always

3 Do you watch TV in bed?

a never   **b** sometimes   **c** always

4 Do you watch TV at meal times?

a never   **b** sometimes   **c** always

5 Does your family say that you watch too much TV?

a never   **b** sometimes   **c** always

READING

1 Read the quiz from a teen magazine and choose your answers.

2 **SPEAKING** Work in pairs. Ask and answer the questions with your partner.

3 Work out your score and read your answer. Do you agree with it?

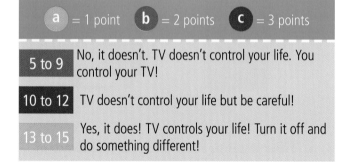

a = 1 point **b** = 2 points **c** = 3 points	
5 to 9	No, it doesn't. TV doesn't control your life. You control your TV!
10 to 12	TV doesn't control your life but be careful!
13 to 15	Yes, it does! TV controls your life! Turn it off and do something different!

GRAMMAR
Present simple (questions)

1 **Look back at the quiz. Put the words in order to make questions. Then complete the rule.**

1 your / TV / life / control / does / ?

2 watch / in / you / TV / bed / do / ?

> **RULE:** We use **do** and **does** [1] *before* / *after* the subject to make questions. We use [2] _____ + I/you/we/they + base form and [3] _____ + he/she/it + base form.
>
> To answer we use:
> Yes, I/you/we/they **do**.   No, I/you/we/they **don't**.
> Yes, he/she/it **does**.   No, he/she/it **doesn't**.

2 **Choose the correct words.**

0 *Do I* *Does* your dad cook?

1 *Do / Does* your best friend play football?

2 *Do / Does* you like pizza?

3 *Do / Does* your parents play computer games?

4 *Do / Does* your teacher give you a lot of homework?

5 *Do / Does* you hang out with your friends after school?

3 **Write questions.**

0 you / watch TV with your family
Do you watch TV with your family?

1 best friend / play tennis

2 your mum and dad / ask for help with housework

3 you / like dogs

4 your mum / take you shopping

5 your friends / listen to music / every day

4 **SPEAKING** Work in pairs. Ask and answer the questions in Exercises 2 and 3.

> *Does your dad cook?*

> *Yes, he does. He sometimes cooks at the weekend.*

> *No, he doesn't. He never cooks.*

Workbook page 47

VOCABULARY
Gadgets

1 🔊 1.58 **Match the gadgets in the list with the pictures. Write 1–8 in the boxes. Listen and check.**

1 e-reader | **2** games console | **3** GPS
4 headphones | **5** laptop | **6** MP3 player
7 smartphone | **8** tablet

A

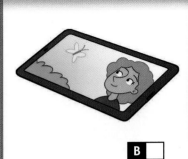

B

C

D

E 1

F

2 SPEAKING **Work in pairs. Tell your partner which of these gadgets you use every day.**

> I use a tablet every day.

> I don't use a laptop every day.

3 SPEAKING **Look at the table and make sentences.**

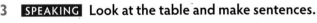

I use / don't use my	tablet games console MP3 player smartphone GPS laptop e-reader headphones	to	play computer games. shop. listen to music. do homework. read books/magazines. talk to my friends. watch TV. find out which way to go.

Workbook page 49

G

H

WRITING
Days in your life

1 🔊 1.59 **Complete the days of the week with the missing vowels. Listen and check.**

M _o_ nd _a_ y
T ___ sd __ y
W __ dn __ sd __ y
Th __ rsd __ y
Fr __ d __ y
S __ t __ rd __ y
S __ nd __ y

2 **What do you do or not do on different days? Choose three days and make notes.**

Sunday   – football
           – no school

3 **Write about three days of the week.**

> I like Sunday because I always play football and I don't go to school. It's a great day.

The school play

1 **Look at the photos and answer the questions.**

Who can you see in the first photograph?
How do Tom and Ellie feel in photo 2?

2 🔊 1.60 **Now read and listen to the photostory. What does Ruby agree to do?**

RUBY Where are Tom and Ellie?
DAN They're at Drama club. They're in the school play, remember?
RUBY Oh, that's right. They're amazing.
DAN What do you mean?
RUBY To be in a play in front of all the school.

1

DAN Look. Here they are. They don't look very happy.
RUBY Hi, guys. What's wrong?
TOM It's Anna Williams. She's in the play but she's ill.
ELLIE We really need her. The play is on Friday.

2

ELLIE I've got an idea. Ruby, do you want to be in the play? You can have Anna's part.
RUBY Me! No way!
TOM Oh, come on, Ruby. Please. We really need you.
DAN Do it, Ruby. Help your friends.

3

RUBY Oh, OK.
ELLIE I love you, Ruby! Thank you so much.
TOM Yes, you're the best.
RUBY Am I crazy?

4

DEVELOPING SPEAKING

3 ◼◀ EP3 **Watch to find out how the story continues.**

Does Ruby do the play?

4 ◼◀ EP3 **Watch again. Correct the false information in the sentences.**

0 Ruby is excited about the play.
Ruby is nervous about the play.
1 It's four days until the performance.
2 In the play, Ruby wants to speak to the queen.
3 Dan has some bad news for Ruby.
4 Anna Williams is ill.
5 Anna doesn't want to be in the play.

PHRASES FOR FLUENCY

1 Find the expressions 1–4 in the story. Who says them?

1 What's wrong?
2 I've got an idea.
3 No way!
4 Oh, come on.

2 How do you say the expressions in Exercise 1 in your language?

3 Put the sentences in the correct order to make a dialogue.

☐	MOLLY	Oh, come on, Ben. Please!
☐	MOLLY	It's my homework. Can you help me with it?
☐	MOLLY	Very funny, Ben.
1	MOLLY	Hi, Ben. Listen. There's a problem.
☐	BEN	No way! I always help you with homework.
☐	BEN	Oh? What's wrong?
☐	BEN	No! But listen – I've got an idea. Ask Mum!

4 Complete the dialogues with the expressions from Exercise 1.

0 A I'm bored.
  B Me too. _____*I've got an idea.*_____ Let's play football in the park.
1 A Can I talk to you? I've got a problem.
  B Really? _____
2 A I don't want to come to the party.
  B Oh, _____ Jenny. Parties are great!
3 A Come to the café with me.
  B _____ I don't like the café.

FUNCTIONS
Encouraging someone

1 Put the words in order to make sentences.

I'm worried. I don't want to do it.

1 are / you / great
2 can / do / it / you
3 worry / don't
4 here / I'm / help / you / to

2 Choose a picture and write a dialogue.

3 SPEAKING **Work in pairs. Act out the dialogue.**

OBJECTIVES

FUNCTIONS: helping a friend; describing people

GRAMMAR: *have / has got* (positive, negative and questions); countable and uncountable nouns

VOCABULARY: parts of the body; describing people

READING

1 Match the things in the list with the photos. Write 1–6 in the boxes.

1 a woman with a child | 2 a shaved head
3 short black hair | 4 green eyes
5 a doctor and a nurse | 6 long curly hair

2 **SPEAKING** Work in pairs. Complete the sentences. Tell your partner.

My eyes are _____ .
My hair is _____ .
My best friend's eyes are _____ .
My mum's hair is _____ .

> My eyes are brown.

3 ◀)) 1.61 Read and listen to the article. What's wrong with Delaney?

4 Read the article again. Match the parts of the sentences.

0 Delaney is 11 and the girls and boys — e
1 The doctors say that she's got
2 She's in hospital for months and this
3 Delaney hasn't got any hair
4 Kamryn shaves her head and
5 The teachers at the school don't want Kamryn

a a terrible illness.
b so Delaney is really happy.
c and her friend Kamryn wants to help her.
d at school with a shaved head.
e in her class like her a lot.
f is difficult for her, but she's strong.

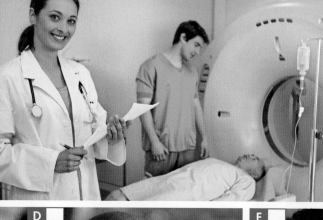

A

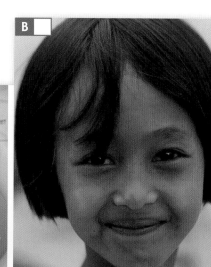

B

C

D

E

F 1

A real friend

Delaney Clements is 11. She's got a big smile and beautiful hair. She's a very active girl and loves sport. Delaney is very popular with her classmates. Her best friend is a girl called Kamryn. She's in Delaney's class.

One day Delaney is very tired and feels bad. Her mum and dad take her to hospital. The doctors check the girl. They say that Delaney is very ill. She's got cancer. Her parents are very worried.

Delaney is in hospital for months. It's a very difficult time for her, but she often smiles. The doctors and nurses like her a lot. She's a very strong girl.

Delaney looks very different now. She hasn't got any hair. But she's got a real friend, Kamryn. Kamryn talks to her parents. She wants to help Delaney. She wants to look like Delaney. Delaney feels different from her classmates. Kamryn shaves her head. When Delaney sees her friend without hair, she's very happy. She's got a really good friend. Now Delaney isn't alone.

But there is a terrible surprise for Kamryn the next day at school. Her teachers say it isn't OK to have a shaved head. They don't want Kamryn to go to school with a shaved head.

A lot of people don't understand the teachers, and they tell the school what they think. The newspapers have got lots of stories about the two girls.

In the end, the teachers say it's OK. Kamryn goes back to school.

THiNK VALUES

Helping a friend

SPEAKING How can you help a friend in these situations? Work in pairs. Use the suggestions in the list and your own ideas.

I help him/her study. | I talk to him/her.
I make him/her a sandwich. | I lend him/her my tablet.
I give him/her a hug.

1 My friend is sad.
2 My friend gets a bad mark in his/her Maths test.
3 My friend is hungry with nothing to eat.
4 My friend's computer is broken.
5 My friend has got a problem at school.

GRAMMAR

have / has got (positive and negative)

1 **Look at the article on page 57. Choose the correct form of *have got* in the sentences. Then complete the rule and the table.**

1 She *'ve got / 's got* a big smile.
2 She *haven't got / hasn't got* any hair.
3 The newspapers *has got / have got* lots of stories about the two girls.

> **RULE:** We use *have / has* (+ *not*) +
> 1 _____ to talk about possession.

Positive	Negative
I/you/we/they**'ve** got (have got)	I/you/we/they 1_____ got (have not got)
he/she/it**'s** got (2_____ got)	he/she/it **hasn't** got (has not got)

2 **Complete the sentences with the correct form of *have got*.**

0 This computer is £700. I __*haven't got*__ the money to buy it.
1 My best friend Tony _____ any sisters, but he _____ two brothers.
2 I _____ a tablet but I really want one.
3 I _____ a new smartphone. Here's my new number.
4 James and Annie _____ a car, but they've got bikes.
5 Lara _____ a big family. She _____ three sisters and one brother.

Workbook page 54

VOCABULARY

Parts of the body

1 🔊 1.62 **Label the picture with the words in the list. Listen and check.**

~~arm~~ | body | ear | eye | face
foot | hand | leg | mouth | nose

2 **SPEAKING** **Work in pairs. Look at the picture and labels for 30 seconds. Then cover the words. Point to the parts of the body and test your partner.**

> What's this?

> It's an arm.

Workbook page 57

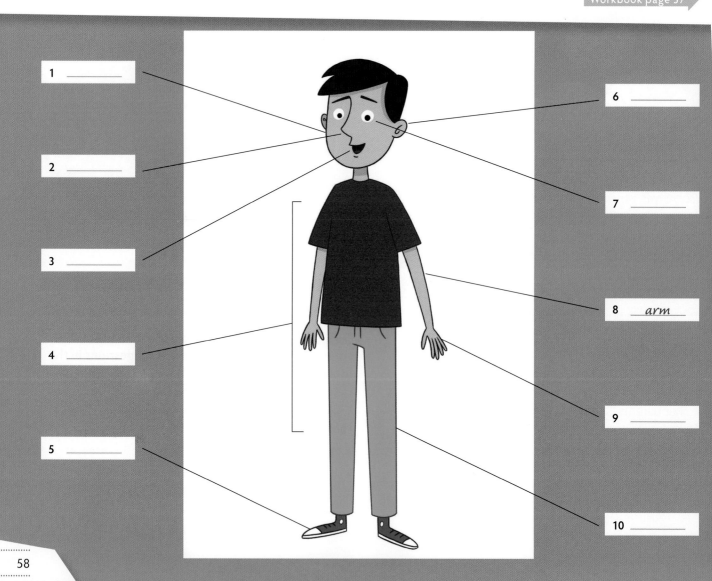

1 _____
2 _____
3 _____
4 _____
5 _____
6 _____
7 _____
8 __*arm*__
9 _____
10 _____

LISTENING

1 Which of these sentences do you agree with?

1 It's good to give little presents to your friends sometimes.
2 A friendship band is a great present.
3 I really like friendship bands.

2 Look at the photo and read the text. Then answer the question.

Why do people like friendship bands?

3 ◀)) 1.63 Listen to an interview with 12-year-old Ella Winston. What are her hobbies?

4 ◀)) 1.63 Listen again and complete the sentences.

0 Ella's got five or six *friendship bands* .
1 She's got two or three _____ .
2 In total, she's got about _____ friends.
3 She spends about _____ a day making friendship bands.
4 The rubber bands are not _____ .
5 Sometimes she uses seven or eight different _____ .

Friendship bands

David Beckham has got one. The Duchess of Cambridge has got one. Harry Styles from One Direction has got one. And millions of other young and old people have got them, too. Friendship bands are popular all over the world. They are fun and look cool. And, they help us to think of our friends.

GRAMMAR

have / has got (questions)

1 Match the questions and answers. Complete the table.

1 Have you got a hobby?
2 Has your sister got a smartphone?
3 Have your teachers got friendship bands?

a Yes, she has.
b No, they haven't.
c Yes, I have.

Questions	Short answers
Have I/you/we/they **got**?	Yes, I/you/we/they **have**. No, I/you/we/they **haven't**. (**have not**)
¹_____ he/she/it **got**?	Yes, she/he/it ² _____ . No, she/he/it ³ _____ . (**has not**)

2 Answer the questions.

1 Have you got a TV in your bedroom?
2 Have you got a TV in your kitchen?
3 Have you got a garden?
4 Have you got a big family?
5 Has your best friend got a big family?
6 Have you got a mobile phone with lots of songs on it?

3 SPEAKING Walk around the classroom. Ask and answer the questions in Exercise 2. Find someone with a 'yes' answer for each question and write down their name.

Countable and uncountable nouns

4 Complete the table with the words in the list and *a/an* or *some*. Then complete the rule.

apple | ~~arm~~ | ~~bikes~~ | chairs | colour | ~~friend~~
fun | hobby | money | pens | ~~time~~ | work

Countable (singular)	Countable (plural)	Uncountable
an arm *a friend*	*some bikes*	*some time*

RULE: You can count **countable** nouns: one, two, three, etc. + **countable** noun (e.g. *two friends, four bikes*).

With singular **countable** nouns, we use *a* or ¹_____ .

You can't count **uncountable** nouns (e.g. *time*).

With **uncountable** nouns and plural **countable** nouns, we use ²_____ .

Workbook pages 54–55

READING

1 🔊1.64 **Read and listen to the dialogue. What's the surprise for Olivia?**

OLIVIA	Hey, Chloe. How are you?
CHLOE	Hi, Olivia. I'm fine. How are you?
OLIVIA	I'm happy. You know my brother, Patrick, right? Well, he's got a new friend. He's really cool.
CHLOE	Really? Who is he? What does he look like?
OLIVIA	Well, he's got black hair. It's short and it's curly.
CHLOE	Is he tall or short?
OLIVIA	Quite tall, and good-looking. He's got brown eyes and he wears glasses.
CHLOE	Brown eyes and glasses?
OLIVIA	Erm … yes, and he's got a very nice smile. He's so friendly.
CHLOE	I know.
OLIVIA	You know?
CHLOE	He likes football and tennis and his name's Freddie, right?
OLIVIA	That's right, but … but …
CHLOE	And he's got a sister?
OLIVIA	How do you know?
CHLOE	Freddie's … my brother!
OLIVIA	No way!

2 **SPEAKING** **Which picture shows Freddie? Tell a partner.**

He's number … He's got …

 1    2    3

VOCABULARY
Describing people (1)

1 **Look at the words in the list. Write them under the correct headings. Some words can go under more than one heading.**

~~blue~~ | ~~grey~~ | ~~long~~ | curly | short | black | blonde
red | brown | wavy | straight | green

eye colour	hair colour	hair style
blue	*grey*	*long*

2 **SPEAKING** **Work in pairs. Use the words in Exercise 1 to describe the people in the photos.**

James Rodriguez

Pink

George Clooney

Shakira

James Rodriguez has got …

Pink has got …

Workbook page 57 ➤

Pronunciation
Long vowel sound /eɪ/
Go to page 120. 🔊

Describing people (2)

3 🔊 1.67 **Match the words in the list with the pictures. Write 1–7 in the boxes. Listen and check.**

1 beard | 2 earring | 3 glasses
4 moustache | 5 short | 6 smile | 7 tall

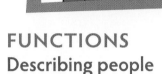

4 🔊 1.68 **Put the words in the correct order to make sentences. Listen and check. Then match each sentence with a picture in Exercise 3.**

0 smile / a / she's / nice / very / got   `F`
   She's got a very nice smile.

1 she / glasses / wears   ☐

2 moustache / got / a / he's   ☐

3 he's / beard / a / got   ☐

4 got / earring / right / she's / her / ear / an / in   ☐

5 is not short / she / quite tall / she's   ☐

5 🔊 1.69 **Complete the dialogue with the missing words. Listen and check.**

A I've got a new friend. His name's Eric.

B What does he look like?

A He's got short brown ⁰h *air*_____ , blue ¹e_____ and he wears ²g_____ .

B Is he tall or ³s_____ ?

A He isn't very tall.

B Is he nice?

A He's very nice and friendly. He's got a nice ⁴s_____ .

6 🗣️ SPEAKING **Work in pairs. Act out the dialogue.**

Workbook page 57 ▶

FUNCTIONS
Describing people

1 Complete the dialogue with answers a–d.

A I'm thinking of a famous footballer.

B What does he look like?

A ⁰ _d_

B What's he like?

A ¹_____

B Is he British?

A ²_____

B Is it Gareth Bale?

A ³_____

a He's really nice.

b Yes, he is.

c Yes, it is.

d He's tall and strong. He's got short brown hair and a lovely smile.

2 🗣️ SPEAKING **Work in pairs. Think of a famous person. Ask and answer questions to guess who he/she is.**

> I'm thinking of a famous female singer.

> What does she look like?

■ TRAIN TO THiNK ■
Attention to detail

1 🗣️ SPEAKING **Work in pairs. Student A: Go to page 127. Student B: Go to page 128. Describe the people in your picture. Find the six differences.**

2 🗣️ SPEAKING **Tell others in the class what differences you have found.**

> In picture A, the waiter has got grey hair. In picture B, ...

Culture

Welcoming people around the world

Western countries

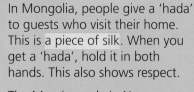

What do you do when you see someone you know? Do you smile? Do you say hello? Do you touch the other person? Here are some ideas for travellers. They tell you how people in different countries and cultures welcome each other. Do you do different things in your country?

In many countries in the East, people bow their heads when they greet each other. This shows respect and in China is called 'kowtow'. In Thailand, people put their hands together and bow. This is called the 'wai'.

When people in Tibet greet each other, they stick out their tongue. This is a very old tradition. But you can still see it in Tibet today.

In Mongolia, people give a 'hada' to guests who visit their home. This is a piece of silk. When you get a 'hada', hold it in both hands. This also shows respect.

The Maori people in New Zealand rub noses together when they meet. This is called the 'hongi'.

In Western countries, many people shake hands when they greet each other. Sometimes they just smile and say something like 'Hello!' or 'Hi!'

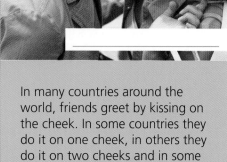

In many countries around the world, friends greet by kissing on the cheek. In some countries they do it on one cheek, in others they do it on two cheeks and in some they kiss cheeks three times.

1 Look at the photos on page 62. Find these things or actions.

bow their heads | kiss | a piece of silk
put their hands together | rub noses
shake hands | stick out their tongue
touch

2 What do the photos show?

A people saying hello
B people helping people
C people saying thank you

3 🔊 1.70 Read and listen to the article. Write the names of the places under the photos.

4 Read the article again. Mark the sentences T (true) or F (false).

0	The 'kowtow' is a tradition in China.	T
1	In Thailand, people rub their noses to say hello.	
2	In Tibet, it is not OK to show someone your tongue.	
3	When you get a 'hada', don't hold it in one hand.	
4	Maori people use the 'hongi' to say hello.	
5	In Western countries, people never shake hands.	
6	People only greet others with a kiss in Western countries.	
7	In some countries, people kiss three times.	

5 **SPEAKING** Discuss with a partner.

1 Which is your favourite way of welcoming people described in the text?
2 How do you welcome people in your country?

WRITING
Describing a friend

1 Read the text. Tick (✓) the correct picture of James.

My best friend is called James Webb. He's quite tall. He's got short curly black hair and he wears glasses. He's in my class at school and he always helps me in my lessons. After school we always play football in the park and at the weekends we often go swimming together. He's a really friendly boy and he's got a very nice smile. He's very popular and everyone likes him. But I'm his best friend!

2 Read the text again. Complete the notes about James.

Appearance: hair – _____ , _____
and _____
wears _____
tall
has got a nice smile

Personality: friendly – (nice smile!)
_____ – (has got lots of friends)

3 Think about your best friend. Make notes.

Appearance:

Personality:

4 Answer the questions about your best friend.

1 What's his/her name?
2 How do you know him/her?
3 Why do you like him/her?
4 What do you do together?

5 Use your notes from Exercises 3 and 4 to write a short text (35–50 words) about your best friend.

■ THiNK EXAMS ■

READING AND WRITING
Part 4: Multiple-choice reading comprehension

1 **Read the article about a school club.**

For each sentence choose the correct answer A, B or C.

Our school has a LEGO club and it's great fun. It's on Tuesday and Thursday lunchtime from 12 pm to 1 pm. I'm a member of the club and so is my best friend Ally.

Mr Thomas is the club organiser and the club is in his classroom, 3T. He's got five big boxes of LEGO bricks.

Every week he spends the first 15 minutes showing us different ways to build things. We then practise this for the rest of the time. He sometimes organises competitions. The prize is always a small box of LEGO.

This month there is a competition for all schools in the UK to build a LEGO classroom. The prize is a school trip to LEGOLAND. I hope our LEGO club wins!

0 The LEGO club is at _____ .
  A the library B the museum Ⓒ school

1 The club meets _____ times a week.
  A two B three C four

2 The meetings are for _____ .
  A 15 minutes B 30 minutes C 60 minutes.

3 Mr Thomas teaches in _____ 3T.
  A school B classroom C box

4 Mr Thomas shows the students how to make things with LEGO for _____ .
  A fifteen minutes B thirty minutes C one hour

5 The prize for Mr Thomas' competition is a _____ .
  A LEGO model B LEGO book C trip to LEGOLAND

Part 9: Guided writing

2 **Read the email from your pen friend Sophie.**

From: Sophie
To:

Please tell me about the things you do in your free time. What do you do after school? What do you do at the weekend?

Write an email to Sophie and answer the questions. Write 25–35 words.

VOCABULARY

1 **Complete the sentences with the words in the list. There are two extra words.**

arm | beard | curly | dance | do | earrings | eyes | glasses | go | headphones | out | short

1 No, I can't go out. I need to _____ my homework.
2 I always use _____ when I listen to music at home.
3 She's got a friendship band on her left _____ .
4 It's OK music, but you can't _____ to it.
5 My eyes aren't very good. That's why I wear _____ .
6 Let's _____ shopping tomorrow afternoon.
7 He's got a big black _____ and a moustache.
8 I like her hair. It's long and _____ .
9 He's got really nice blue _____ .
10 I want to go and hang _____ with my friends this evening.

/10

GRAMMAR

2 **Put the words in order to make sentences or questions.**

1 like / shopping / she / doesn't
2 never / they / to / listen / rock music
3 many / got / you / DVDs / haven't
4 she / money / got / has / lots of
5 always / I / late / to school / get
6 lots / got / you / of / have / books
7 usually / are / tired / on Sunday evenings / we

3 **Find and correct the mistake in each sentence.**

1 I go often to the cinema.
2 They listen not to music.
3 He play computer games all the time.
4 Have he got a moustache?
5 She don't do her homework.
6 I've got a work to do tonight.
7 You have got a big family?

/14

FUNCTIONAL LANGUAGE

4 **Write the missing words.**

1 A There's a new girl in our class.
  B Oh? What's she _____ ?
  A She's nice. But she _____ talk a lot.
  B Oh. And what does she _____ like?
  A She's tall and she's got long black hair.

2 A Are you OK?
  B No. I can't do this homework.
  A Don't _____ . I can help you.
  B Oh, thanks. You're _____ !
  A No problem. I'm here to _____ you.

/6

MY SCORE /30

| 22 – 30 |
| 10 – 21 |
| 0 – 9 |

PRONUNCIATION

UNIT 1
/h/ or /w/ in question words

1 🔊 1.18 **Read and listen to the questions.**

How old are you?
Where are you from?
What's your favourite food?
Who's your favourite football player?
Why do you like him?

2 **Say the question words in blue.**

3 🔊 1.19 **Listen again and repeat. Then practise with a partner.**

UNIT 2
Vowel sounds – adjectives

1 🔊 1.27 **Read and listen to the dialogue.**

TOM   Mum's **hungry**.
JANE   Mum? But why? Why is she **angry**?
TOM   I said Mum's **hungry**. She wants a sandwich.
JANE   Oh, … OK. Well, Dad's **angry**.
TOM   Does he want a sandwich, too?
JANE   No! I said he's **angry**.

2 **Which sounds are different in *hungry* and *angry*? Say them and make the differences clear.**

3 🔊 1.28 **Listen again and repeat. Then practise with a partner.**

UNIT 3
this / that / these / those

1 🔊 1.36 **Read and listen to the dialogue.**

ANNA   Can I have **that** cake, please?
ASSISTANT   **This** one or **that** one?
ANNA   **That** one – the chocolate one.
ASSISTANT   **That's** a fruitcake, but **these** cupcakes are chocolate.
ANNA   Oh! Can I have two of **those**, then?
ASSISTANT   Of course. Here you are.

2 **Say the words *that*, *this*, *those* and *these*.**

3 🔊 1.37 **Listen again and repeat. Then practise with a partner.**

UNIT 4
Word stress in numbers

1 🔊 1.47 **Read and listen to the dialogue.**

TIM   It's my sister's birthday today. She's **thirteen**.
JULIE   **Thirty**! That's old!
TIM   **Thirty**? No! I said, '**Thirteen**'.
JULIE   Oh, … thirteen. She's the same age as me.

2 **Where is the stress on the red words? Where is the stress on the blue words?**

3 🔊 1.48 **Listen again and repeat. Then practise with a partner.**

UNIT 5
Present simple verbs – third person

1 🔊 1.54 **Read and listen to the sentences.**

Liz **catches** the bus to school every morning.
She **teaches** French at a secondary school.
At 4.30 she **finishes** work.
After dinner, Liz **washes** the dishes.
Before she goes to bed, she **chooses** her clothes for the next day.

2 **How many syllables are there in *catch*? How many syllables are there in *catches*? Say the words in blue.**

3 🔊 1.55 **Listen again and repeat. Then practise with a partner.**

UNIT 6
Long vowel sound /eɪ/

1 🔊 1.65 **Read and listen to the dialogue.**

CUSTOMER   I'm sorry I'm **late**. I have a table for 1.00.
WAITER   That's **okay**. But **Jane Grey's waiting** for you.
CUSTOMER   OK. But I don't know her. Is she the girl there, with the long **straight** hair?
WAITER   No. Her hair's **wavy** and **grey**.
CUSTOMER   Oh! The woman with the pink **face**? The one eating **cake**?
WAITER   Yes, that's her. I'll **take** you to the **table**.

2 **Say the words in blue. Which vowel sound do they all have?**

3 🔊 1.66 **Listen again and repeat. Then practise with a partner.**

This page is intentionally left blank.

GET IT RIGHT!

UNIT 1
Be

> Learners often miss out *am*, *are* or *is* in sentences.
>
> We use the subject + *be* + object.
> ✓ *I'm from Spain.*
> ✗ *I from Spain.*
>
> In questions, we use *be* + subject + object + question mark.
> ✓ *Are they from Scotland?*
> ✗ *They from Scotland?*

Tick ✓ the correct sentences and cross ✗ the incorrect ones. Correct the mistakes.

0 He my favourite athlete.   ✗
   He is my favourite athlete.
1 The house very nice.
2 How old you?
3 I'm from Edinburgh.
4 You 13 years old?
5 What your name?
6 My favourite singer is Sam Smith.
7 My name John.
8 Lisbon in Spain?

Subject pronouns and *be*

> Learners sometimes miss out the subject pronoun when using *be*.
>
> We always use the subject + *be*.
> ✓ *This is Mike. He is from England.*
> ✗ *This is Mike. Is from England.*

Correct the mistakes in the sentences.

0 I like Maria. Is very funny.
   I like Maria. She is very funny.
1 I like England. Is very nice.
2 It's a taxi. Is yellow.
3 She's my friend. Is from Mexico.
4 They are singers. Are in First Aid Kit.
5 He's my brother. Is 15 years old.
6 I like this phone because is very small.

UNIT 2
Be questions

> Learners make mistakes with word order in *be* questions.
>
> In positive sentences, we use subject + *be*. In questions, we use the order *be* + subject + (object) followed with a question mark (?).
> ✓ *That is OK.*
> ✓ *Is that OK?*
> ✗ *That is OK?*

Put the words in the correct order to make questions.

0 it / expensive / is ?
   Is it expensive?
1 there / is / problem / a ?
2 on / holiday / are / you ?
3 how / you / are ?
4 a / is / famous person / he ?
5 computer game / this / is / your ?
6 she / is / sister / your ?

Spelling

> Learners sometimes have trouble spelling words in English.
> ✓ *That is my pencil.*
> ✗ *That is my pensil.*

Correct the spelling mistakes in the sentences.

0 She is my frind.
   She is my friend.
1 My brother is very funy.
2 The food is excelent.
3 My shirt is withe.
4 We play football in the evining.
5 I saw her yesterday moring.
6 The film is greate.

UNIT 3
Possessive 's

Learners find it difficult to use possessive 's. They often put the words in the wrong order.

We use person + possessive 's + thing/person.

✓ This is my brother's car.
✗ This is ~~the car of my brother.~~

Rewrite the sentences using possessive 's.

0   I went to the house of my cousin.
    I went to my cousin's house.
1   It is the homework of my sister.
2   The name of my friend is Amy.
3   I was at the party of my friend.
4   The family of my friend lives in India.
5   It is the birthday of my sister.
6   This is the bedroom of my brother.
7   Trumpington High is the school of my cousin.
8   Don't eat the burger of Juan!
9   That's the chair of the teacher.
10 He's the brother of Ana.

Family vocabulary

Learners sometimes make spelling mistakes with family words.

✓ This is my cousin Jean.
✗ This is my ~~cousine~~ Jean.
✗ This is my ~~couzin~~ Jean.

Correct the spelling mistakes in the family words.

0   How is your familly?
    How is your family?
1   My mather is in hospital.
2   We go to my granmother's house.
3   I watch films with my borther.
4   It was a present from my fater.
5   He is the president's sun.
6   He has got two daugthers.
7   My granfather lives there.
8   She is my cousine.
9   His family are form America.
10 Does your uncel live near you?

UNIT 4
There is / There are

Learners sometimes miss out *there* where *there is/are* is required.

We use *there* + *be* + noun, where *be* agrees with the noun. We do not use *there have* or *there has*.

✓ There is a great café on this street.
✗ ~~Is a great café~~ on this street.
✗ ~~There has a great café~~ on this street.

Correct the mistakes in the sentences.

0   Next week is a party.
    Next week there is a party.
1   In the kitchen are two windows.
2   In Paris there has a nice park.
3   Are any other drinks?
4   In my room there has a bed.
5   It is nice because are lots of shops.
6   Near my town there have lots of interesting places.

Prepositions of place

Learners sometimes make mistakes with the form of prepositions of place, either misspelling them or using the wrong particle.

✓ The shop is next to the post office.
✗ The shop is ~~next the post office.~~

Correct the mistakes in the sentences.

0   My house is oposite the school.
    My house is opposite the school.
1   The coffee shop is infront of the bank.
2   My house is nex to Park Hotel.
3   I live behing the station.
4   Station Road is beetween the supermarket and the post office.
5   The shop is opposit the museum.
6   Their houses are next the hospital.

UNIT 5
Present simple positive

> Learners often make agreement mistakes in the present simple.
>
> ✓ *It helps me with my studies.*
> ✗ *It ~~help~~ me with my studies.*

Correct the mistakes in the sentences.

0 He play football.
   He plays football.
1 He eat breakfast every day.
2 They likes sports.
3 She go to university.
4 Angela work Monday to Friday.
5 People plays games on their phones.
6 School start on Friday.
7 People in cities is often angry.
8 He studyies every day after school.
9 She love Glee Club.
10 My brother watchs football on TV every Saturday.

Present simple negative

> Learners sometimes make agreement mistakes in the present simple negative.
>
> The verb *do* agrees with the person and number of the subject.
>
> ✓ *He doesn't like sports.*
> ✗ *He ~~don't~~ like sports.*

Choose the correct options in the sentences.

0 They (don't)/ *doesn't* understand.
1 She *doesn't / don't* have any time.
2 He *doesn't / don't* like sweets.
3 We *doesn't / don't* need to wear tennis clothes.
4 It *don't / doesn't* cost much.
5 My teacher *don't / doesn't* give me a lot of homework.
6 I *don't / doesn't* like computer games.
7 I *don't / doesn't* play sports after school.
8 You *don't / doesn't* go to my school.
9 My brother *don't / doesn't* help me with my homework.
10 Planes *don't / doesn't* fly to our city.

UNIT 6
Countable and uncountable nouns

> Learners sometimes confuse *a(n)* with *some*.
>
> We use *a* or *an* with countable nouns in the singular. We use *some* for countable nouns in the plural.
>
> ✓ *We can buy a present for his birthday.*
> ✗ *We can buy ~~some present~~ for his birthday.*
> ✓ *We can buy some presents for his birthday.*
>
> We also use *some* with uncountable nouns.
>
> ✓ *You need some water.*
> ✗ *You need ~~a water~~.*

Choose the correct options in the sentences.

0 I've got *some /*(a)T-shirt.
1 We took a break and ate *some / a* sandwich.
2 The best present was *some / a* jacket.
3 I have got *some / a* good news.
4 Can you take *some / a* photo of us?
5 I listen to *some / a* nice music with my family.
6 He has got *some / a* good friends.

has / have got

> Learners often forget to include *got* when they use *has / have got* in negative sentences and questions.
>
> ✓ *Has he got a dog?*
> ✗ *Has he a dog?*
> ✓ *He hasn't got a bike.*
> ✗ *He hasn't a bike.*

Correct the mistakes in the sentences

0 I haven't any sisters
   I haven't got any sisters
1 Have you the time?
2 Has your mum GPS in her car?
3 I haven't headphones. Can I use yours?
4 They haven't books in their school. They use tablets.
5 I haven't an e-reader. I use my phone.
6 Have you a laptop?

STUDENT A

UNIT 4, PAGE 43, VOCABULARY

Student A

Ask and answer the questions with your partner.

How much is the smartphone?

It's ...

How much are the ...?

They're ...

UNIT 6, PAGE 61, TRAIN TO THINK

Student A

Describe to your partner what the people in your picture look like. Your partner describes what the people in his/her picture look like. Find the six differences.

STUDENT B

UNIT 4, PAGE 43, VOCABULARY

Student B

Ask and answer the questions with your partner.

£200.00

£15.00

€8.50

€3.80

How much is the TV?

It's ...

How much are the ...?

They're ...

UNIT 6, PAGE 61, TRAIN TO THINK

Student B

Describe to your partner what the people in your picture look like. Your partner describes what the people in his/her picture look like. Find the six differences.

Acknowledgements

The authors and publishers acknowledge the following sources of copyright material and are grateful for the permissions granted. While every effort has been made, it has not always been possible to identify the sources of all the material used, or to trace all copyright holders. If any omissions are brought to our notice, we will be happy to include the appropriate acknowledgements on reprinting.

The publishers are grateful to the following for permission to reproduce copyright photographs and material:

T = Top, B = Below, L = Left, R = Right, C = Centre, B/G = Background

p.5 (TL): © Zoonar GmbH / Alamy; p.5 (TC): Foodcollection / Getty Images; p.5 (TR): Peshkova / Getty Images; p.5 (TL): fStop Images / Getty Images; p.5 (TC): © Ivan Vdovin / Alamy; p.5 (TR): © Michael Dwyer / Alamy; p.5 (CL): vsl / Shutterstock; p.5 (CL): © YAY Media AS / Alamy; p.5 (CR): © Rrrainbow / Alamy; p.5 (CL): © RTimages / Alamy; p.5 (CB): © Nadiya Teslyuk / Alamy; p.5 (BR): © The Picture Pantry / Alamy; p.5 (BC): © Tetra Images / Alamy; p.5 (BL): © russ witherington / Alamy; p.5 (BC): © Tom Grundy / Alamy; p.5 (BR): © Tetra Images / Alamy; p.7 (TL): Kali Nine LLC / Getty Images; p.7 (BL): © Tetra Images / Alamy; p.7 (TR): Steve Smith / Getty Images; p.7 (CR): Marcus Mok / Getty Images; p.7 (BR): Hill Street Studios / Getty Images; p.8 (TL): Datacraft Co Ltd / Getty Images; p.8 (TR): © Archideaphoto / Alamy; p.8 (TL): © Zoonar GmbH / Alamy; p.8 (TR): © Dmitry Rukhlenko / Alamy; p.8 (TR): © aviv avivbenor / Alamy; p.8 (TL): Hemera Technologies / Getty Images; p.8 (CL): © Anton Starikov / Alamy p.8 (CL): koya79 / Getty Images; p.8 (CL): © Héctor Sánchez / Alamy; p.8 (CR): © RTimages / Alamy; p.11 (BL): © Ivan Kmit / Alamy; p.11 (BL): © Robert Kneschke / Alamy; p.11 (BC): © Mark Sykes / Alamy; p.11 (BR): © Dmitry Rukhlenko / Alamy; p.11 (BR): © arkela / Alamy; p.13 (TR): © AHowden - Brazil Stock Photography / Alamy; p.13 (TL): © Cavan Images / Alamy; p.13 (BR): © Tiziana and Gianni Baldizzone/CORBIS; p.13 (BL): SensorSpot / Getty Images; p.15 (TR): © Action Plus Sports Images / Alamy; p.15 (TR): Jordi Ruiz / Getty Images; p.15 (TR): © infusny-244/INFphoto. com/Corbis;p.15 (TR): © ROBIN UTRECHT FOTOGRAFIE/HillCreek Pictures/ Corbis; p.15 (TR): © Sydney Alford / Alamy; p.19 (BR): Wavebreakmedia Ltd / Getty Images; p.20 (TC): JGI/Jamie Grill / Getty Images; p.20 (TL): © Sandra Baker / Alamy; p.20 (TC): KevinCarr / Getty Images; p.20 (TC): Alexander Hafemann / Getty Images; p.20 (TR): Tom Merton / Getty Images; p.20 (TR): © Jaak Nilson/ Spaces Images/Corbis; p.24 (TL): © ZUMA Press, Inc. / Alamy; p.24 (TR): Tom Hahn / Getty Images; p.24 (TC): Jstone / Shutterstock; p.24 (TL): © Miguel Aguirre Sánchez / Alamy; p.24 (TR): © Jason Smalley Photography / Alamy; p.26 (TL): Danita Delimont / Gallo Images / Getty Images; p.26 (TR): Rolf Hicker / Getty Images; p.26 (CL): © Robbie Jack/Corbis; p.26 (BR): © Janine Wiedel Photolibrary / Alamy; p.26 (BR): © Miles Davies / Alamy; p.26 (BL): Piotr Krzeslak / Shutterstock; p.27 (BL): © Hero Images/Corbis; p.27 (BR): © Phil Boorman/Corbis; p.30 (TL): © BRETT GARDNER / Alamy; p.30 (TR): Amble Design / Shutterstock; p.30 (C): Wavebreak Premium / Shutterstock; p.30 (CR): © Blend Images / Alamy; p.31 (TL): AFP / Stringer / Getty Images; p.31 (TR): Mario Testino /Art Partner / Getty Images Publicity; p.31 (CR): © Peter Scholey / Alamy; p.32 (TL): © Denys Kuvaiev / Alamy, p.32 (TL): © Cavan Images / Alamy; p.32 (CL): © incamerastock / Alamy; p.32 (CL): © Gregg Vignal / Alamy; p.32 (BL): © Juice Images / Alamy; p.32 (BL): © Johner Images / Alamy; p.32 (CR): Jose Luis Pelaez Inc / Getty Images; p.32 (CR): JGI/ Jamie Gril / Getty Images; p.32 (CR): Hero Images / Getty Images; p.32 (CR): Jose Luis Pelaez Inc / Getty Images; p.32 (CR): Tanya Constantine / Getty Images; p.32 (CR): Maria Teijeiro / Getty Images p.32 (CR): JGI/Jamie Grill; p.32 (CR): Streetfly

Studio/JR Carvey / Getty Images; p.32 (CR): Jose Luis Pelaez Inc / Getty Images; p.35 (CL): sagir / Shutterstock; p.35 (CL) © Maksym Bondarchuk / Alamy; p.35 (CL): Sebastian Meckelmann / Getty Images; p.35 (CL): © Maksym Bondarchuk / Alamy; p.35 (CL): © Yongyut Khasawaong / Alamy; p.35 (CL): © Stocksolutions / Alamy; p.35 (CL): Mosquito / DigitalVision Vectors / Getty Images; p.35 (CL): © Oleksiy Maksymenko / Alamy; p.37 (CR): Westend61 / Getty Images; p.38 (BL): © imageBROKER / Alamy; p.38 (BL): © Helen Sessions / Alamy; p.38 (BR): © Robert Harding Picture Library Ltd / Alamy; p.38 (BR): © Dave G. Houser/Corbis; p.39 (TR): © imageBROKER / Alamy; p.39 (TC): © Felix Hug/Corbis; p.39 (BR): © Atlantide Phototravel/Corbis; p.42 (TL): © Gordon Shoosmith / Alamy; p.44 (TR): Roc Canals Photography / Getty Images; p.44 (TL): © CW Images / Alamy; p.44 (TR): © Krystyna Szulecka / Alamy; p.44 (TL): Insight Photography / Design Pic / Getty Images; p.44 (TL): © GerryRousseau / Alamy; p.44 (TC): Jon Arnold / Getty Images; p.44 (CR): bluehand / Shutterstock; p.45 (CL): © Ian Dagnall Commercial Collection / Alamy; p.45 (B): VisitBritain/Rod Edwards / Getty Images; p.48 (TL): © Auslöser/Corbis; p.48 (TR): Tara Moore / Getty Images; p.48 (BL): © mainpicture / Alamy; p.48 (BR): © Elvele Images Ltd / Alamy; p.48 (TL): Charlotte Nation / Getty Images; p.48 (BR): © redsnapper / Alamy; p.50 (TR): © David J. Green - Lifestyle / Alamy; p.50 (TR): Syda Productions / Shutterstock; p.50 (TR): Uwe Umstatter / Getty Images; p.50 (TR): Tetra Images / Getty Images; p.50 (TR): Blend Images - KidStock; p.50 (TR): Alex Segre / Getty Images; p.51 (TL): luismmolina / Getty Images; p.51 (TL): © RTimages / Alamy; p.51 (TL): Juffin / Getty Images; p.51 (TL): pictafolio / Getty Images; p.56 (TL): Avatar_023 / Getty Images; p.56 (TC): Peathegee Inc / Getty Images; p.56 (TR): © Hugh Sitton/Corbis; p.56 (TR): © dbimages / Alamy; p.56 (C): © Keith Levit / Alamy; p.56 (C): Xavier Arnau / Getty Images; p.57 (T): Fuse / Getty Images; p.57 (L): Renee Eppler / Getty Images; p.57 (R): Stephan Kaps / EyeEm / Getty Images; p.59 (TR): Veena Nair / Getty Images; p.60 (TL): © Tetra Images / Alamy; p.60 (CR): © ZUMA Press, Inc. / Alamy; p.60 (CR): © ZUMA Press, Inc. / Alamy; p.60 (CR): Debby Wong / Shutterstock; p.60 (CR): JB Lacroix / WireImage / Getty Images; p.62 (TC): © ONOKY - Photononstop / Alamy; p.62 (TR): © Blaine Harrington III / Alamy; p.62 (C): © MELBA PHOTO AGENCY / Alamy; p.62 (C): Blend Images - Noel Hendrickson / Getty Images; p.61 (BL): Philip Game / Getty Images; p.61 (BC): © Craig Lovell / Eagle Visions Photography / Alamy; p.61 (BR): © Kim Steele/Blend Images / Corbis; p.64 (TR): Skip Odonnell / Getty Images; p.64 (BL): © Niels Poulsen / Alamy; p.127 (TL): © Erik Reis / Alamy; p.127 (TL): alexey_boldin / Getty Images; p.127 (TL): © Digifoto Green / Alamy; p.127 (TL): © Aydin Buyuktas / Alamy; p.127 (TL): © D. Hurst / Alamy; p.127 (TL): pictafolio / Getty Images; p.127 (BL): © Newscast-online Limited / Alamy; p.127 (BL): © Konstantin Gushcha / Alamy.

Commissioned photography by: Mike Stone p 18, 36, 54.

Cover photographs by: (L): ©Tim Gainey/Alamy Stock Photo; (R): ©Yuliya Koldovska/Shutterstock;

The publishers are grateful to the following illustrators: Christos Skaltsas (hyphen) 4, 6, 9, 14, 15, 16, 17, 22, 23, 33, 34, 40, 43, 46, 52, 53, 55, 58, 60, 61, 63, 127, 128 and Zaharias Papadopoulos (hyphen) 8, 12, 21, 35, 41, 63.

The publishers are grateful to the following contributors:
hyphen: editorial, design and project management; Leon Chambers: audio recordings; Silversun Media Group: video production; Karen Elliott: Pronunciation sections; Matt Norton: Get it Right! sections

This page is intentionally left blank.

WORKBOOK STARTER

A1

Herbert Puchta, Jeff Stranks & Peter Lewis-Jones

CAMBRIDGE
UNIVERSITY PRESS

This page is intentionally left blank.

CONTENTS

WELCOME

The alphabet

1 ◀)02 Listen and write the names and the cities.

Names

0 *H a r r y*

1 _ _ _ _

2 _ _ _ _ _ _

3 _ _ _ _

4 _ _ _ _ _ _

5 _ _ _ _ _

Cities

1 _ _ _ _ _ _

2 _ _ _ _ _ _

3 _ _ _ _ _ _ _

4 _ _ _ _ _ _

5 _ _ _ _ _

6 _ _ _ _ _ _

2 Match to make the words.

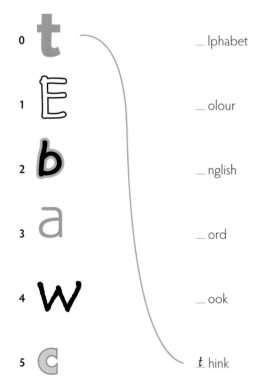

0 **t**   _ lphabet

1 E   _ olour

2 **b**   _ nglish

3 a   _ ord

4 **W**   _ ook

5 c   *t* hink

Colours

1 ◀)03 Listen and write the colours. Then colour.

0 *b l a c k*

6 _ _ _ _ _ _

1 _ _ _

7 _ _ _ _

2 _ _ _ _ _

8 _ _ _ _

3 _ _ _ _ _

9 _ _ _ _ _ _

4 _ _ _ _

10 _ _ _ _

5 _ _ _ _ _

2 Find and (circle) eleven colours in the word snake.

greenorangeblackgreyblueredpurplepinkbrownwhiteyellow

International words

1 Unscramble the letters to make words.

0 trapior *airport*

1 sub _____

2 facé _____

3 -fiiw _____

4 ishus _____

5 bolaotfl _____

6 rbumagerh _____

7 thole _____

8 iytc _____

9 openh _____

10 zizap _____

11 tranaurest _____

12 cinadswh _____

13 axit _____

14 inevilesto _____

15 bleatt _____

2 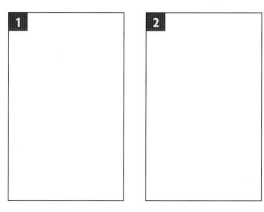 04 **Listen and put the words in order.**

a ☐ hamburger
b ☐ airport
c ☐ phone
d ☐ pizza
e ☐ café
f ☐ television
g ☐ tablet
h 1 sushi
i ☐ hotel
j ☐ city

SUMMING UP

1 05 **Listen and draw.**

1	2

3	4

5	6

Articles: *a* and *an*

1 (Circle) the correct options.

0 *a* / *an* orange bus
1 *a* / *an* Italian city
2 *a* / *an* American TV
3 *a* / *an* white tablet
4 *a* / *an* English actor
5 *a* / *an* hamburger
6 *a* / *an* black taxi
7 *a* / *an* phone
8 *a* / *an* grey airport
9 *a* / *an* red bus

2 Write the words in the list in the correct columns. How many more words can you write?

actor | airport | apple | ~~city~~ | hamburger
hotel | orange | TV

a	an
city	

The day

1 Look at the pictures and complete the phrases.

0 Good *morning*   1 Good _ _ _ _ _ _

2 Good _ _ _ _ _ _ _ _   3 Good _ _ _ _ _ _ _ _ _ _

Saying *Hello* and *Goodbye*

1 Write the words in the list under the pictures.

Bye | Good afternoon | Good evening | Good morning | Good night | ~~Hello~~ | Hi | See you

_____ *Hello* _____   _____   _____   _____

_____   _____   _____   _____

Classroom objects

1 Match the pictures with the words in the list. Write 1–10 in the boxes.

1 ~~book~~ | 2 chair | 3 computer | 4 desk
5 door | 6 pen | 7 pencil | 8 projector
9 board | 10 window

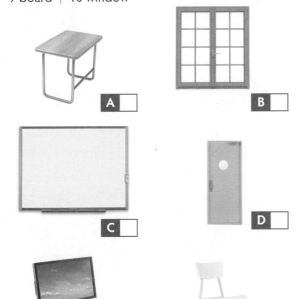

A [ ]   B [ ]

C [ ]   D [ ]

E [ ]   F [ ]

G [ ]   H [ ]

I [ ]   J [1]

2 Find the words from Exercise 1 in the word search.

```
W  B  I  T  T  B  O  A  R  D
I  B  O  V  N  O  W  T  O  P
N  O  I  R  Q  O  M  K  T  E
D  P  Y  T  D  K  B  L  C  N
O  L  S  T  B  Z  K  S  E  D
W  N  V  M  I  Q  G  J  J  U
E  S  R  E  T  U  P  M  O  C
X  J  O  V  C  H  A  I  R  Z
L  R  O  L  I  C  N  E  P  M
G  S  D  H  X  E  K  L  Q  B
```

SUMMING UP

1 🔊 06 Put the dialogues in order. Then listen and check.

Dialogue 1

[1] CONNOR   Good morning, Mr Davis.

[ ] CONNOR   I'm fine. And you?

[ ] MR DAVIS   Hello, Connor. How are you?

[ ] MR DAVIS   I'm great, thanks.

Dialogue 2

[ ] LEWIS   Yeah, have a good day.

[ ] LEWIS   Bye, Paula.

[ ] PAULA   Bye, Lewis. See you later.

Dialogue 3

[ ] LUCY   I'm fine, thank you.

[ ] LUCY   Bye, Mrs Edwards.

[1] LUCY   Good afternoon, Mrs Edwards.

[ ] MRS EDWARDS   Good. I'll see you in class.

[ ] MRS EDWARDS   Hello, Lucy. How are you?

2 Write short dialogues.

OLIVIA   *Hello.* _____

JIM   _____

BRIAN   _____

OLIVIA   _____

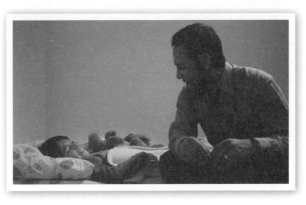

TIM   _____

DAD   _____

Numbers 0–20

1 Write the numbers in the boxes.

1	four	4	12	seven	
2	eight		13	sixteen	
3	twenty		14	eighteen	
4	five		15	ten	
5	twelve		16	fourteen	
6	six		17	three	
7	eleven		18	thirteen	
8	one		19	seventeen	
9	fifteen		20	two	
10	nineteen		21	nine	
11	zero				

Plural nouns

1 How many? Find, count and write the plurals.

book | chair | child | computer | door | ~~man~~
pencil | pen | phone | window | woman

0	eight	_men_
1	three	
2	seven	
3	fifteen	
4	eighteen	
5	two	
6	one	
7	zero	
8	twelve	
9	four	
10	six	

Classroom language

1 (Circle) the correct options.

0 *Close your books. /*
   What does this mean?

1 *Put up your hand. /*
   Close your books.

2 *Listen. /*
   That's right.

3 *Work with a partner. /*
   That's wrong.

4 *Listen. /*
   Look at the picture.

5 *Work with a partner. /*
   Put up your hand.

6 *Open your books. /*
   Look at the picture.

Numbers 20–100

1 Write the numbers.

0	seventy	70
1	thirty	
2	forty	
3	ninety	
4	a hundred	
5	fifty	
6	twenty	
7	sixty	
8	eighty	
9	thirty-four	
10	sixty-eight	
11	twenty-one	
12	ninety-nine	
13	fifty-three	

2 ◀))07 **Listen and write the numbers.**

a _thirty-four_

b _____

c _____

d _____

e _____

f _____

g _____

h _____

i _____

j _____

k _____

Messages

1 ◀))08 **Listen to the messages and (circle) the correct options.**

Message 1

Hi, Luke

Message from Paul [1]*Jones / James* .
His house number is [2]*7 / 8*.
The bus number is [3]*8 / 9*.
His phone number is [4]*0987868758 / 0987886758*.

Message 2

Hi, Debbie

Message from [5]*Claire / Clare* [6]*Green / Greene*.
Her house number is [7]*44 / 34*.
The bus number is [8]*15 / 16*.
Her phone number is
01244 [9]*7564453 / 5634453*.

SUMMING UP

1 ◀))09 **Listen and complete the messages.**

Message 1

Hi, Martin

Message from Mr [0] _Cleverly_ .
His house number is [1] _____ .
The bus number is [2] _____ .
His phone number is [3] _____

Message 2

Hi, Chloe

Message from Jane [4] _____ .
Her house number is [5] _____ .
The bus number is [6] _____ .
Her phone number is [7] _____

1 | ONE WORLD

GRAMMAR
Question words SB page 14

1 ★ ☆ ☆ Complete the sentences with the correct question words.

> 0 __*What*__ is your name?

> 1 _____ old are you?

> 2 _____ are you from?

> 3 _____ is your favourite athlete?

> 4 _____ is he/she your favourite athlete?

2 ★★★ Write answers to the questions in Exercise 1 so they are true for you.

0 *My name is* _____
1 _____
2 _____
3 _____
4 _____

Pronunciation
/h/ or /w/ in question words
Go to page 118. 🔊

3 ★★ ☆ Look at the pictures and (circle) the correct words.

0 *He /* (*She*) */ It* is happy.

1 *We / You / I* are friends.

2 *They / We / You* are Japanese.

3 *She / He / It* is eleven.

4 *I / She / We* am Carla.

5 *We / They / You* are Fred.

6 *We / You / They* are sisters.

7 *I / It / You* is the Brazilian flag.

to be SB page 15

4 ★☆☆ **Complete the table with the words in the list.**

~~am~~ | are | are | are | is | is | is

0	I	*am*	Paul.
1	You		13.
2	He		happy.
3	She		from Mexico.
4	It		Japanese.
5	We		sisters.
6	They		friends.

5 ★★☆ **Complete the sentences with the verb *to be*. Use short forms.**

0 You _____*'re*_____ Russian.

1 I _____ Portuguese.

2 We _____ Mexican.

3 They _____ Brazilian.

4 He _____ Spanish.

5 She _____ American.

6 ★★☆ **Rewrite the sentences using short forms.**

0 It is a Turkish flag.
   It's a Turkish flag.

1 She is Russian.
   _____

2 You are a good friend.
   _____

3 They are British.
   _____

4 We are from London.
   _____

5 I am Paul. What is your name?
   _____

6 He is 12 today.
   _____

GET IT RIGHT! ◉

Subject–verb agreement with *be*

We use the form of *be* that agrees with the subject.

✓ *They **are** from Italy.*

✗ *They **is** from Italy.*

Correct the sentences.

0 There are a beautiful beach.
   There is a beautiful beach.

1 The lessons is for two hours.
   _____

2 It are cold today.
   _____

3 Are the English player good?
   _____

4 We's from France.
   _____

5 My favourite country are the USA.
   _____

VOCABULARY

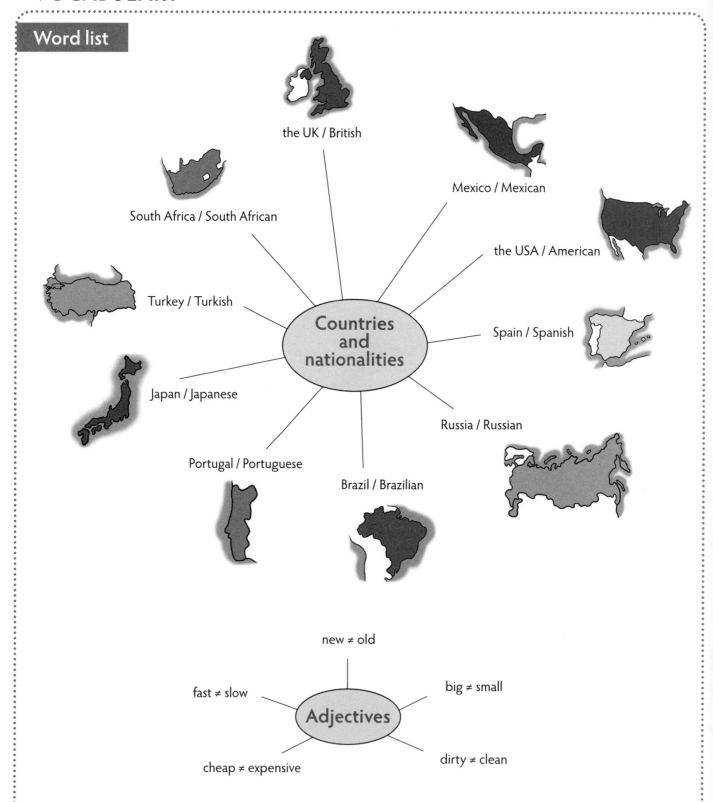

the UK / British

Mexico / Mexican

the USA / American

South Africa / South African

Spain / Spanish

Turkey / Turkish

Countries and nationalities

Japan / Japanese

Russia / Russian

Portugal / Portuguese

Brazil / Brazilian

new ≠ old

fast ≠ slow

Adjectives

big ≠ small

cheap ≠ expensive

dirty ≠ clean

Key words in context

athlete	Usain Bolt is a famous **athlete** from Jamaica.
country	Mexico is a beautiful **country**.
fan	I'm a great **fan** of Jennifer Lawrence.
flag	The American **flag** is red, white and blue.
nationality	What's your **nationality**?
player	Gareth Bale is my favourite football **player**.

Countries and nationalities
SB page 14

1 ★☆☆ **Find ten countries in the word search. Then write the countries.**

N	H	I	S	O	C	I	X	E	M
I	B	R	A	Z	I	L	S	G	E
A	B	V	J	A	S	K	O	J	T
K	C	N	A	M	P	S	U	I	U
U	Y	E	I	F	A	L	T	C	R
E	M	Z	S	E	S	L	H	G	K
H	P	B	S	K	P	R	A	H	E
T	H	E	U	S	A	U	F	X	Y
A	C	V	R	W	I	Z	R	B	J
E	J	A	P	A	N	A	I	T	Q
R	R	K	A	Y	H	B	C	N	M
G	P	O	R	T	U	G	A	L	D

0 _Brazil_

1 _____

2 _____

3 _____

4 _____

5 _____

6 _____

7 _____

8 _____

9 _____

2 ★★☆ **Complete the words.**

0 Oliver's from Cape Town. He's South Afric_an_ .

1 He's from London. He's Briti_____ .

2 I'm from Mexico City. I'm Mexic_____ .

3 She's from New York. She's Americ_____ .

4 They're from Barcelona. They're Span_____ .

5 You're from Moscow. You're Russi_____ .

6 My mum is from Rio. She's Brazili_____ .

7 Our teacher is from Lisbon. He's Portugu_____ .

8 Haruki is from Tokyo. He's Japan_____ .

9 They're from Istanbul. They're Turk_____ .

Adjectives
SB page 17

3 ★☆☆ **Write the adjectives under the pictures.**

big | cheap | clean | dirty | ~~expensive~~
fast | new | old | slow | small

The car is …

0 _expensive_ .

1 _____ .

2 _____ .

3 _____ .

4 _____ .

The car is …

5 _____ .

6 _____ .

7 _____ .

8 _____ .

9 _____ .

4 ★★☆ **Put the words in order to make sentences.**

0 book / English / My / new / is
  My English book is new.

1 red / Her / is / pen

  _____

2 is / house / old / Our

  _____

3 fast / bikes / Their / are

  _____

4 big / school / Our / is

  _____

5 My / small / bedroom / is

  _____

6 car / Her / expensive / is

READING

1 REMEMBER AND CHECK Complete the table. Then look at the website on page 13 of the Student's Book and check your answers.

Name	Age	Country	City	Favourite athlete
Pedro	*10*			
Brittany				
Oleg				
Haruka				

2 Read the text quickly. Where are they from? Match the names with the countries.

0	Juan	*c*	a	Turkey
1	Mary Lou		b	South Africa
2	Ibrahim		c	Mexico
3	Rebecca		d	the USA
4	Lucy		e	the UK

— □ ✕

Hi, my name's Juan. I'm from Acapulco. I'm Mexican. I'm twelve years old.
My favourite athlete is James Rodriguez. He's a football player from Colombia. He's great.

My name's Mary Lou. I'm ten years old. I'm American. I'm from Dallas.
My favourite athlete is Rafael Nadal. He's a tennis player. He's Spanish. He's awesome.

Hi, I'm Ibrahim. I'm from Istanbul. I'm Turkish. I'm eleven years old.
My favourite athlete is Ellie Simmonds. She's a swimmer from the UK. She's really fast.

My name's Rebecca. I'm twelve years old. I'm South African. I'm from Cape Town.
My favourite athlete is Marta. She's a footballer. She's Brazilian. She's amazing.

My name's Lucy. I'm eleven years old. I'm British. I'm from Liverpool.
My favourite athlete is Usain Bolt. He's a runner. He's Jamaican. He's great.

3 Read the text again. Mark the sentences T (true) or F (false).

0	Juan is from Mexico City.	*F*
1	Juan's favourite athlete is a football player.	
2	Mary Lou is ten.	
3	Mary Lou's favourite athlete is a Brazilian tennis player.	
4	Ibrahim is from Turkey.	
5	Ellie Simmonds is an American swimmer.	
6	Rebecca is eleven.	
7	Rebecca is from Brazil.	
8	Lucy is from Liverpool.	
9	Lucy's favourite athlete is a woman.	

DEVELOPING WRITING

About me

1 Read the mini questionnaire. Then complete the text with the missing words.

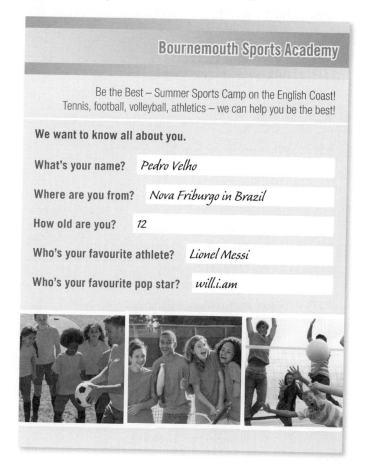

Bournemouth Sports Academy

Be the Best – Summer Sports Camp on the English Coast!
Tennis, football, volleyball, athletics – we can help you be the best!

We want to know all about you.

What's your name? *Pedro Velho*

Where are you from? *Nova Friburgo in Brazil*

How old are you? *12*

Who's your favourite athlete? *Lionel Messi*

Who's your favourite pop star? *will.i.am*

Hi, my name is ⁰_____ *Pedro* _____.
I'm Brazilian. I'm from ¹_____.
I'm ²_____ years old.
My favourite athlete is
³_____.
He's a football player from Argentina.
He's amazing. I love football!
I love music, too. My favourite pop star is
⁴_____. He's awesome.

2 Use the text to complete the questionnaire.

Hi, my name is Amy Davies. I'm American.
I'm from Seattle. I'm eleven years old.
My favourite athlete is Serena Williams.
She's a tennis player from the USA.
She's awesome. I love tennis!
I love music, too. My favourite pop star
is Taylor Swift. She's great.

Bournemouth Sports Academy

Be the Best – Summer Sports Camp on the English Coast
Tennis, football, volleyball, athletics – we can help you be the best!

We want to know all about you.

What's your name? ⁰ *Amy Davies*

Where are you from? ¹_____

How old are you? ²_____

Who's your favourite athlete? ³_____

Who's your favourite pop star? ⁴_____

3 Complete the text about you.

Hi, my name is ¹_____ . I'm ²_____ . I'm from ³_____ .
I'm ⁴_____ years old. My favourite athlete is ⁵_____ . He's / She's a
⁶_____ from ⁷_____ . He's / She's ⁸_____ . I love ⁹_____ !
I love music, too. My favourite pop star is ¹⁰_____ . He's / She's ¹¹_____ .

LISTENING

1 🔊 **12** Listen to the dialogue. Number the people in the order you hear them.

☐

☐

1

☐

☐

2 🔊 **12** Listen again and write the names in the list under the pictures in Exercise 1.

Ayse | Keiko | Kayla | Roberto | Steve

3 Circle the correct answers (A or B).

0 Keiko is from …
  A Japan.   B Lisbon.
1 Roberto is from …
  A Beijing.   B Lisbon.
2 Ayse is from …
  A Istanbul.   B Moscow.
3 Steve is from …
  A London.   B Cape Town.
4 Kayla is from …
  A London.   B Cape Town.

DIALOGUE

1 Choose the correct answers (A, B or C) to complete the dialogue.

BOY   Hi, what's your name?
GIRL I'm 0 A 12.
            B Brazil.
          Ⓒ Julia.
BOY   And where are you from?
GIRL 1 A I'm American.
         B I'm 10.
         C Sara.
BOY   What city are you from?
GIRL 2 A Japan.
         B New York.
         C Mexico.
BOY   New York's a beautiful city.
GIRL 3 A Yes, I am.
         B Yes, it is.
         C Yes, they are.
BOY   Who's your favourite singer?
GIRL 4 A Pharrell Williams.
         B Ronaldo.
         C Yes.
BOY   Why is he your favourite singer?
GIRL 5 A No.
         B Yes.
         C Because he's awesome.
BOY   Nice to meet you, Julia.
GIRL 6 A Yes.
         B No.
         C Nice to meet you, too.

PHRASES FOR FLUENCY SB page 19

1 Match the phrases 1–4 with their similar meanings a–d.

1 How's it going?   ☐   a Goodbye.
2 See you later.   ☐   b How are you?
3 I know.   ☐   c Great.
4 That is so awesome!   ☐   d You're right.

2 Use the phrases 1–4 in Exercise 1 to complete the dialogues.

1 A Hi, Connor. _____
  B I'm fine, thanks.

2 A Bye, Janice.
  B Bye, Tim. _____

3 A This is my new laptop.
  B _____

4 A Liam's a great football player.
  B _____

Sum it up

The Big World Quiz

1 Where do you find these things?

1
A the USA
B the UK
C Spain

2
A the USA
B Turkey
C Russia

3
A Mexico
B Brazil
C Japan

4
A Japan
B Portugal
C Spain

3 Where are these capital cities?

1 Lisbon
   A Portugal
   B Brazil
   C Mexico
2 Pretoria
   A the UK
   B Japan
   C South Africa
3 Ankara
   A the USA
   B Turkey
   C Spain
4 Brasilia
   A Mexico
   B Russia
   C Brazil

2 Where do they say 'hello' like this?

1 'How's it going?'
   A the USA
   B Portugal
   C Brazil
2 'Buenos Dias'
   A Spain
   B Turkey
   C the UK
3 'Konnichiwa'
   A Russia
   B South Africa
   C Japan
4 'Merhaba'
   A Russia
   B Turkey
   C Mexico

4 Who is from …

1 Brazil?
   A Marta
   B Tony Kroos
   C James Rodriguez
2 the UK?
   A Serena Williams
   B Usain Bolt
   C Ellie Simonds
3 Russia?
   A Bruno Mars
   B Maria Sharapova
   C will.i.am
4 the USA?
   A Taylor Swift
   B Gareth Bale
   C Lionel Messi

ANSWERS 1 1B 2A 3B 4A **2** 1A 2A 3C 4B **3** 1A 2C 3B 4C **4** 1A 2C 3B 4A

2 I FEEL HAPPY

GRAMMAR

to be (negative, singular and plural)

SB page 22

1 ★☆☆ Circle the correct form of *to be*.

0 Joe *is* / *am* happy today. It *'s* / *'re* his birthday.

1 We *am* / *are* excited. We *'s* / *'re* on holiday.

2 It *'s* / *'m* late. I *'s* / *'m* tired.

3 Helen and Amanda *is* / *are* happy today. They *is* / *are* in the tennis team.

4 You *are* / *is* angry.

5 It *is* / *are* hot here.

2 ★★☆ Complete the sentences with the correct negative form of *to be*.

0 I ___*'m not*___ tired. I'm worried.

1 James _____ happy. He's bored.

2 Sarah and Jane _____ worried. They're excited.

3 We _____ angry with you. We're worried about you. That's all.

4 Susan _____ happy at her new school. Her new classmates _____ very friendly.

5 It _____ hot in here. It's cold. Close the window.

6 I _____ hungry. I'm thirsty.

to be (questions and short answers)

SB page 23

3 ★★☆ Circle the correct form of *to be*.

1 A *Is* I / *Are* Martin and Matt with you?
   B No, they *isn't* / *aren't*.

2 A *Am* / *Is* I in your team?
   B Yes, you *is* / *are*.

3 A *Am* / *Are* you on the beach now?
   B No, we *isn't* / *aren't*.

4 A *Is* / *Are* Nick at home?
   B No, he *isn't* / *aren't*.

5 A *Is* / *Are* Emma at school today?
   B Yes, she *is* / *are*.

6 A *Am* / *Are* you American?
   B No, I *'m not* / *aren't*.

4 ★★☆ Write the questions. Then write answers to the questions so they are true for you.

0 your name / Mary?
   Is your name Mary?   *No, it isn't.*

1 you / 15?
   _____   _____

2 you / Mexican?
   _____   _____

3 your mum / a teacher?
   _____   _____

4 your dad / from England?
   _____   _____

5 you / happy?
   _____   _____

6 your / classmates / friendly?
   _____   _____

5 ★★☆ Complete the text messages with the correct form of *to be*.

Hi, Kathy. 0 ___*Are*___ you happy?
1 _____ your new school OK?
2 _____ the students friendly?
3 _____ it sunny there? It
4 _____ (✗) sunny here ☹.
School 5 _____ (✗) the same
without you ☹. Text me.

Hi, Marie. I 6 _____ (✓) happy ☺.
School 7 _____ (✓) very different
here in Australia. There 8 _____ (✓)
ten boys and twelve girls in my class.
The girls 9 _____ (✓) very friendly
but the boys 10 _____ (✗) ☹.
It 11 _____ (✓) very hot and sunny
here ☺. And guess what? There
12 _____ (✓) a swimming pool in
the playground ☺. It 13 _____ (✗)
all bad!

Object pronouns `SB page 25`

6 ★☆☆ **Complete the sentences with** *me*, *him*, *her*, *us*, *you* **and** *them*.

My new school

0   My new school is excellent. I really like
     _____*it*_____ .

1   The school dinners are great. I like _____ .

2   Our English teacher is Mrs Smith. I like
     _____ .

3   We are good students. Mrs Smith is very happy
     with _____ .

4   Tim is my best friend here. He's great. I really like
     _____ .

5   I'm friendly. My classmates like _____ .

6   Are you friendly? Do your classmates like
     _____ ?

7 ★★☆ **Complete the dialogues so they are true for you. Use the correct object pronouns.**

0   A   Do you like _____*Neymar*_____ ? (name of a sports
            person)
     B   Yes, I really like _____*him*_____ .

1   A   Do you like _____ ? (name of a girl
            singer)
     B   Yes, I like _____ . She's great.

2   A   Do you like _____ ? (name of pop
            group)
     B   No, I don't like _____ . They're terrible.

3   A   Do you like _____ ? (name of an actor)
     B   Yes, I like _____ . He's an excellent actor.

4   A   Do you like _____ ? (name of a film)
     B   Yes, I like _____ . It's very funny.

8 ★★★ **Write questions with** *like* **and the word in brackets. Then write answers to the questions so they are true for you.**

0   Katy Perry? (you)
     Do you like Katy Perry?
     Yes, I like her. She's a great singer.

1   the TV programme *Dr Who*? (you)
     _____
     _____

2   football? (your dad)
     _____
     _____

3   One Direction? (your best friend)
     _____
     _____

4   Taylor Swift? (you)
     _____
     _____

5   comedy films? (your mum)
     _____
     _____

6   the song 'Good Feeling' by Flo Rida? (you)
     _____
     _____

7   talent shows? (your mum and dad)
     _____
     _____

GET IT RIGHT! 👁
Object pronouns

We use *it* **in the singular and** *them* **in the plural**

✓ *I don't want this sweet. You have **it**.*

✓ *I don't want these sweets. You have **them**.*

✗ *I don't want these sweets. You have **it**.*

Ⓒircle **the correct options.**

0   This is my school. I like *it* / *them*.

1   I play computer games. I like *it* / *them*.

2   My dad has a really cool phone. I want *it* / *them*!

3   My country is small but I like *it* / *them* a lot.

4   One Direction? I don't like *it* / *them*.

5   My friends are here. I play football with *it* / *them*
     every afternoon.

6   Here is my homework. I finished *it* / *them* this
     morning.

VOCABULARY

Adjectives to describe feelings

cold

sad

bored

hot

worried

angry

hungry

excited

tired

thirsty

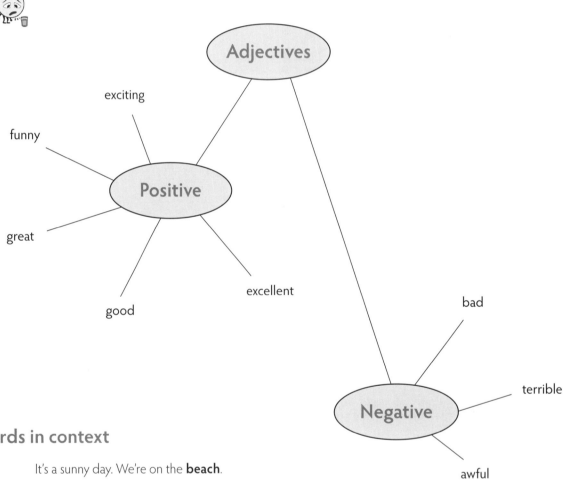

Key words in context

beach	It's a sunny day. We're on the **beach**.
bus	I'm on the **bus** with my friends.
club	It's a **club**. They do lots of different activities there.
film	I like comedy **film**s. They're funny.
friendly	I like Kate. She's very **friendly**.
holiday	My friend is on **holiday** in Australia.
mask	My mum's carnival **mask** is very beautiful.
song	I love the **song** 'Royals' by Lorde.
stadium	I'm at the **stadium**. There's a football match today.
sweets	I like chocolate and **sweets**.
team	Mike is in our football **team**.
train	We're on the **train** with my mum.

Adjectives to describe feelings
SB page 22

1 ★☆☆ Unscramble the letters to make adjectives.

0 r e d i t   _tired_

1 x c e t i e d   _ _ _ _ _ _ _

2 o r r w i e d   _ _ _ _ _ _ _

3 y a n g r   _ _ _ _ _

4 o r b e d   _ _ _ _ _

5 o h t   _ _ _

6 s t y i r t h   _ _ _ _ _ _

7 d a s   _ _ _

8 d l o c   _ _ _ _

9 g r y n u h   _ _ _ _ _ _

2 ★★☆ Complete the sentences with the adjectives in Exercise 1.

0 It's late and you're _tired_ . Go to bed.

1 My new bike is broken. My dad's _____ with me.

2 I'm _____ . Let's play a game on your tablet.

3 My friends are _____ . There's a football match at our school today.

4 There's an exam at school today. Simon's _____ .

5 Andy's dog is ill. He's _____ .

6 I'm hot and _____ . Can I have a drink?

7 He's _____ . He wants a sandwich.

8 It's winter. It's _____ .

9 We're _____ . Let's go for a swim!

3 ★★★ Circle the correct adjectives.

0 A Are you _worried_ / excited about the exam tomorrow?

   B No, I'm not. It's an easy exam.

1 A Is Kate _excited_ / _bored_ about the holiday?

   B Yes, she is.

2 A It's _cold_ / _hot_ today. Let's go for a swim.

   B Yes, OK. That's a good idea.

3 A Are you _hungry_ / _thirsty_?

   B Yes, I am.

   A Let's have some pizza then.

4 A It's really _hot_ / _cold_ in here.

   B You're right. Let's close the window.

5 A I'm really _tired_ / _thirsty_.

   B Here's a bottle of water.

   A Thanks.

6 A Mum's _angry_ / _sad_ with you.

   B Why?

   A You're late home.

Positive and negative adjectives
SB page 25

4 ★★☆ Unscramble the words and complete the sentences.

0 He's a _bad_ actor. (dba)

1 She's a _____ player. (ogod)

2 São Paulo is a _____ city. (arget)

3 The weather today _____ . (fluwa)

4 It's a _____ game. (unfyn)

5 There's an exam today. It's _____ ! (ritlerbe)

6 The pizzas here are _____ . (etnlcxele)

7 Volleyball is an _____ sport. (igecntix)

5 ★☆☆ Complete the sentences so they are true for you.

0 _Shakira_ is a great singer.

1 _____ is a good book.

2 _____ is a funny actor.

3 _____ is a terrible sport.

4 _____ is a great football player.

5 _____ is an exciting city.

6 _____ is an awful computer game.

7 _____ is a bad song.

8 _____ and _____ are excellent games.

6 ★★☆ Complete the dialogues so they are true for you. Use _Yes, I do_ or _No, I don't_ and an adjective from the list.

awful | bad | excellent | exciting
funny | good | ~~great~~ | terrible

0 A Do you like football?

   B _Yes, I do_ . It's a(n) _great_ sport.

1 A Do you like swimming?

   B _____ . It's a(n) _____ sport.

2 A Do you like the Harry Potter books?

   B _____ . They're _____ books.

3 A Do you like basketball?

   B _____ . It's a(n) _____ game.

4 A Do you like Ronaldo?

   B _____ . He's a(n) _____ football player.

5 A Do you like _The Hobbit_ films?

   B _____ . They're _____ films.

Pronunciation
Vowel sounds – adjectives
Go to page 118.

READING

1 REMEMBER AND CHECK Complete the sentences with *likes* or *doesn't like*. Then look at the dialogue on page 24 of the Student's Book and check your answers.

0 Nick _doesn't like_ Formula One.

1 Connor _____ Ben Stiller.

2 Nick _____ him.

3 Nick _____ One Direction.

4 Nick _____ ice cream.

5 Nick _____ Jenny Carter.

2 Read the profile of a famous singer quickly. Find and <u>underline</u> the answers to these questions.

1 What's her real name?

2 What's her stage name?

Name: Ella Yelich-O'Connor
Stage Name: Lorde
Nationality: New Zealander
Place of Birth: New Zealand
Likes: photography, music and books

The year is 2013. Ella Yelich-O'Connor is at secondary school. She's a sixteen-year old teenager from New Zealand. Her mother's name is Sonja Yelich and she's Croatian. Her father's name is Vic O'Connor and he's Irish. Ella is a famous singer, and her hit 'Royals' is at the top of the New Zealand charts. Her first album is in the top five in the UK, Canada, the USA, Ireland and Norway. Maybe it's a hit in your country, too! Ella Yelich-O'Connor is a queen of pop. She likes electronic music and she really likes hip hop.

She's a style icon but does she like fashion?
Yes, she does. She loves clothes.

Does she like social media?
Yes, she does. She likes Twitter and Instagram.

What does she like?
Ella likes books – all kinds of books. Books are important to her. The words of her songs are from books and her songs are like short stories.

---

3 Read the profile again and write short answers to the questions.

0 Is her stage name Ella?   _No, it isn't._

1 Does she like photography?   _____

2 Is Lorde from New York?   _____

3 Is her father Irish?   _____

4 Is she a singer?   _____

5 Does she like electronic music? _____

6 Does she like clothes?   _____

7 Are books important to her?   _____

8 Is she popular in your country? _____

DEVELOPING WRITING

A text message

1 Read the text messages and <u>underline</u> the adjectives.

a

> Hi, Amy. Are you still bored? Read a book! My favourite book is *Anne of Green Gables*. It's a great story. I really like Anne. She's friendly and funny. It's a happy story ☺. Please read it.
> Kate

b

> Hi, Matt. I'm at the cinema. The film is terrible. I don't like it. The actors are very bad. I don't like them. I'm really bored ☹. Where are you? Text me.
> Tim

c

> Hi, James. Are you at home? Listen to this song. It's great. The singer is excellent. The guitarist is good. I really like the song. Do you like it? Text me.
> Lara

d

> Hi, Sally. Thank you for the film. It's very funny. I really like it. My sister likes it too.
> Jim Carrey is great. He's a very funny actor. The other actors are good, too. Speak soon.
> Hannah

e

> Hi, Tony. The song is terrible. The singer is awful. How is it number 1? I don't like it. My friends don't like it. Do you like it?
> Jake

2 Write the adjectives in Exercise 1 in the correct columns.

Positive	Negative
	bored

3 Look at the text messages in Exercise 1. Use *likes* or *doesn't like* to complete the sentences.

0   Kate ___*likes*___ the book. It's a ___*happy*___ story.

1   Tim _____ the film. It's _____ .

2   Lara _____ the song. It's _____ .

3   Hannah _____ the film. It's _____ .

4   Jake _____ the song. It's _____ .

4 You like a book and you want to text a friend about it. Complete the text message.

> Hi, _____ . Are you still bored? Read a book! My favourite book is _____ . It's a _____ story. I really like _____ . He/She is _____ . It's a _____ story. Please read it.

5 You don't like a film and you want to text a friend about it. Complete the text message.

> Hi, _____ . I'm at the cinema. The film is _____ . I _____ it. The actors are _____ . I _____ them. I'm really _____ ☹. Where are you? Text me.

6 Think about a film, a book, a band or a song and write notes about it.

> Title: _____
> like / don't like   great / terrible
> _____
> _____
> _____

Writing tip: Some useful language

I *like* / *don't like* the film.
I really *like* / *love* the film.
The *film* / *book* / *band* / *song* is *funny* / *exciting* / *sad*.
The *actor(s)* / *singer(s)* *is* / *are great* / *terrible* / *awful*.
The ending is *happy* / *sad*.

7 Now write a short text message about the film, book, band or song. Write 35–50 words.

LISTENING

1 🔊 **15** Listen to the dialogues. Which dialogue (1–5) matches the photo?

2 🔊 **15** Listen again and mark the sentences T (true) or F (false).

1 It's Emma's birthday.   `T`

2 Tom is cold. ☐

3 John doesn't like English. ☐

4 Tim doesn't like the film. ☐

5 Helen's cat is ill. ☐

3 🔊 **15** Listen again and (circle) the correct options.

1 A Hi, Jane.
   B Oh, hi, Kate.
   A It's Emma's birthday today. Is she *happy /* ⟨*excited*⟩?
   B Yes, she is. I'm *happy / excited*, too.

2 A What's the matter?
   B It's *hot / cold* in here. Are you *hot / cold*, Tom?
   A *No, I'm not. / Yes, I am.* I'm wearing a jumper.
   B Well, I'm very *hot / cold*. Can you *open / close* the window?
   A OK.

3 A There's an exam tomorrow. Are you worried, John?
   B No, I'm not worried about it. I *like / don't like* English. I'm just tired.
   A Well, I'm worried. I'm very worried. I *like / don't like* English.

4 A What's wrong, Tim? Are you *tired / bored*?
   B No, I'm not. I'm just *tired / bored*. I don't like this film.
   A Why? I *like / don't like* it. It's very funny.

5 A What's the matter with Helen? Why is she *sad / angry*?
   B Her cat's ill. It's at the vet.
   A Oh, no. That's *sad / terrible*. Poor Helen.

DIALOGUE

1 Complete the dialogue with the words in the list.

don't like | funny | great | ~~likes~~
likes | terrible

A Do you like the song 'Let it Go' from the film *Frozen*?

B No, I don't. But my little sister ⁰___*likes*___ it. It's her favourite song. She sings it all the time. In fact, she ¹_____ all the songs to the film.

A Do you like the film?

B No, I don't. It's ²_____ .
I ³_____ animation films.

A Ah, I really like it. It's a ⁴_____ film. It's
⁵_____ .

▰▰ TRAIN TO THiNK ▰▰

Categorising

1 Put the words in the list into categories. There are four words for each category.

beach | Brazil | ~~cold~~ | New Zealand | sad
school | ~~stadium~~ | ~~the USA~~ | theatre
thirsty | tired | Turkey

Countries	Feelings	Places
the USA	cold	stadium

2 Put words in these three categories.

Nationalities	Colours	Classroom things

3 Name the categories.

1	2	3
good	fourteen	Lara
great	sixty-three	Tim
terrible	one hundred	Katy

Skimming

Reading tip

- Read the questions first. Then read the text quickly.
- Think about what type of text it is. Is it a newspaper article? A letter or an email? A text message?
- Underline the 'important' words, such as adjectives, nouns and verbs.
- Try to answer *Wh-* questions – *Who, What, When* and *Where.*

1 Skim the text in Exercise 4. What type is it?

A a newspaper article

B an email

C a text message

2 Find and write these 'important' words from the text.

two emotions

_____

_____

two positive adjectives

_____

_____

two negative adjectives

_____

_____

3 Complete the table with information about the text.

Who?	
What?	
When?	
Where?	

4 Read the text again and choose the correct answers (A or B).

⊖ ◻ ✕ ◀ ▶ ⌂

Hi, Tess,

I'm bored. It's my little brother Tim's birthday today. He's eight. He's very excited. All his friends are here. It's hot and sunny. They're in the garden now. His friends from his school football team are here. So of course, they all like football. His favourite team is Chelsea. I like Chelsea, too. They're an excellent team.

Guess what his present from me is? It's a Chelsea football! Oh, and a book – *Henry Hunter and the Beast of Snagon*. It's a great story and I really like the pictures. They're excellent.

His presents from Mum and Dad are a bike and a DVD. It's a really good bike but the film is terrible. It's called *Dumb and Dumber*. I don't like it. It isn't funny ☹.

It's 11 am – Tim's birthday lunch is in an hour. But I'm hungry now. There's a big birthday cake ☺.

See you soon,

Samantha

0 Is Samantha excited?

   A Yes, she is.

   (B) No, she isn't.

1 Is it her brother's birthday today?

   A Yes, it is.

   B No, it isn't.

2 Is it a hot day?

   A Yes, it is.

   B No, it isn't.

3 Samantha _____ Chelsea.

   A likes

   B doesn't like

4 *Henry Hunter and the Beast of Snagon* is a/an _____ book.

   A awful

   B great

5 Samantha doesn't like the *Dumb and Dumber* films. They _____ funny.

   A are

   B aren't

6 Is Samantha thirsty?

   A Yes, she is.

   B No, she isn't.

CONSOLIDATION

LISTENING

1 🔊 **16 Listen to Annie and ⬭(circle) the correct answers (A, B or C).**

1 Annie is from …

A

    the USA

B

    South Africa

C

    Mexico

2 She's …

  A 12.   **B** 13.   **C** 14.

3 Her best friend is from …

A

    Brazil

B

    South Africa

C

    the UK

4 Her best friend is called …

  A Paulo.

  B Pedro.

  C Marcel.

2 🔊 **16 Listen again and mark the sentences T (true) or F (false).**

1 Annie is from Cape Town. ☐

2 She doesn't like sport. ☐

3 Her favourite athlete is a tennis player. ☐

4 Her favourite singer is Taylor Swift. ☐

5 Her best friend is Spanish. ☐

6 Her best friend is the same age as her. ☐

VOCABULARY

3 **Complete the sentences with the words in the list. There are two extra words.**

angry | exciting | expensive | fast | hungry | Japan
Japanese | old | Russian | terrible | thirsty | tired

1 Piano lessons aren't cheap. They're _____ .

2 Yuka is from Japan. She's _____ .

3 Dmitri is from Moscow. He's _____ .

4 The car isn't _____ . It's very slow.

5 My phone is _____ . It isn't new.

6 Dad is _____ . He isn't happy.

7 It's very late. I'm very _____ . Good night.

8 Water? Yes, please. I'm really _____ .

9 The new Bond film is really good. It's so _____ !

10 The Italian restaurant is bad. The food is _____ .

GRAMMAR

4 **Complete the dialogues with the missing words.**

1 **A** Do 0 ___*you*___ like ice cream?

   B Yes, I love 1_____ .

2 **A** 2_____ you like dogs?

   B No, I don't like 3_____ .

3 **A** Do you like Lucy?

   B Yes, I like 4_____ . 5_____ is my best friend.

4 **A** Do you like Mr Henderson?

   B No, I don't like 6_____ . 7_____'s boring.

5 **Complete the sentences with the correct form of to be. Use contracted forms.**

0 I _*'m not*_ (✗) Spanish. I __*'m*__ Portuguese.

1 I _____ (✗) ten years old. I _____ eleven.

2 **A** _____ David happy?

   B No, he _____ .

3 Henry and Sally _____ from Australia.

4 **A** _____ you hungry?

   B Yes, we _____ .

5 Maria _____ (✗) twelve. She _____ eleven.

6 **A** Why _____ you angry?

   B Because you _____ late.

7 **A** How old _____ they?

   B Kevin _____ five and Sally _____ eight.

8 **A** Where _____ Ella from?

   B She _____ from South Africa.

DIALOGUE

6 Put the dialogue in order

☐	IZZY	I'm great. It's my birthday today.
☐	IZZY	I know. I'm really excited.
☐	IZZY	Bye.
☐	IZZY	Thanks. I'm off to the new pizza restaurant.
1	IZZY	Hi, Simon, how's it going?
☐	SIMON	Well, have fun. See you later.
☐	SIMON	That is so awesome! Happy Birthday!
☐	SIMON	Oh, hi, Izzy. I'm fine. How about you?
☐	SIMON	The new pizza restaurant? It's great.

READING

7 Read the text and complete the information in the form.

Personal information

Name: 0 _Brad Armstrong_

Age: 1 _____

Nationality: 2 _____

Likes: 3 _____

Favourite athlete: 4 _____

Favourite singer: 5 _____

Best friend: 6 _____

My name is Brad Armstrong. I'm 13 years old.
I'm from the USA. I live in Dallas.
I really like sport. I like basketball and football. My
favourite athlete is Tim Howard. He's a football player.
He's a goalkeeper and he's great.
I also like music. My favourite singer is Ed Sheeran.
He's a British singer. He's really good.
My best friend is Lisa. She's 13 and she's in my school.

8 Read the text again and correct the sentences.

0 Brad is from the UK.
Brad is from the USA.

1 Brad's home town is Chicago.

_____

2 Brad really likes rugby.

_____

3 Tim Howard is a tennis player.

_____

4 Brad's favourite singer is a woman.

_____

5 Brad's best friend is a boy.

_____

6 Lisa is 12.

_____

7 Lisa isn't in his school.

_____

WRITING

9 Write a short text about you. Use the questions to help you. Write 35–50 words.
- What is your name?
- How old are you?
- Where you are from and what is your nationality?
- What do you like?
- Who is your favourite athlete?
- Who is your favourite singer?
- Who is your best friend?

_____

_____

_____

_____

_____

_____

_____

_____

_____

_____

_____

3 | ME AND MY FAMILY

GRAMMAR

Possessive 's SB page 32

1 ★★☆ Follow the lines and complete the sentences. Use 's.

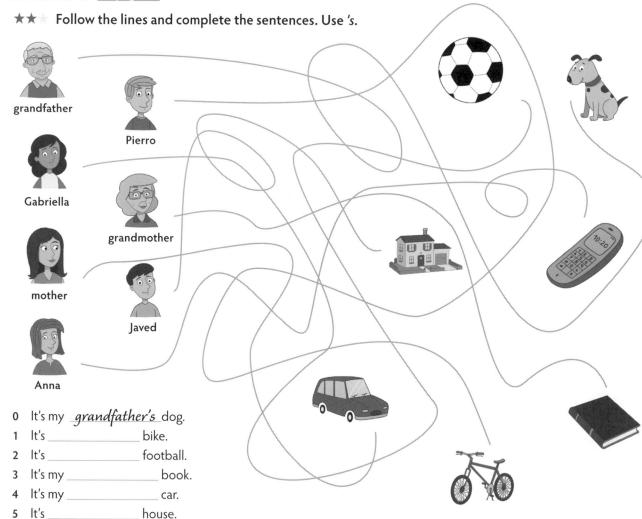

0 It's my _grandfather's_ dog.
1 It's _____ bike.
2 It's _____ football.
3 It's my _____ book.
4 It's my _____ car.
5 It's _____ house.
6 It's _____ phone.

Possessive adjectives SB page 33

2 ★☆☆ Complete the table.

	Possessive adjective
I	my
you	
he	
she	
we	
they	

3 ★★☆ Jake and Sally are at a birthday party. (Circle) the correct possessive adjectives.

JAKE Hi! What's ¹*your / his* name?

SALLY Sally.

JAKE Is that girl ²*her / your* friend?

SALLY Well, no. That's ³*my / their* sister. ⁴*His / Her* name's Marie. This is ⁵*our / your* house.

JAKE Oh. And those two boys?

SALLY They're ⁶*your / my* brothers. They're twins. They're twelve today. It's ⁷*their / our* birthday party. Wait a minute. Who are you?

JAKE I'm Jake. I'm with Mark. I'm ⁸*her / his* cousin.

SALLY Oh, right.

4 ★★☆ **Complete the sentences.**

0 It's George's dog. It's _____his_____ dog.
1 It's my mother's book. It's _____ book.
2 They're Jenny's sweets. They're _____ sweets.
3 It's Penny and Kate's apartment. It's _____ apartment.
4 It's my brother's and my TV. It's _____ TV.
5 They're John's CDs. They're _____ CDs.
6 It's my grandfather's chair. It's _____ chair.
7 I have three cousins – that's _____ house.
8 That's my family's car. It's _____ car.
9 A Is that _____ phone on the table?
   B No, this is _____ phone in my hand.
10 A Is _____ name Nina?
    B No, _____ name is Lara.

this / that / these / those SB page 34

5 ★★☆ (Circle) **the correct answers (A, B or C).**

0 _____ is my bedroom.
  (A) This   B These   C Those
1 _____ is my new MP3 player.
  A Those   B That   C These
2 _____ are photos of my cat.
  A That   B These   C This
3 _____ computer on the table is my sister's.
  A Those   B These   C That
4 Are _____ your books over there?
  A these   B that   C those
5 Is _____ a good film?
  A these   B this   C those
6 _____ boys are from Brazil.
  A This   B That   C Those
7 _____ hotel is very expensive.
  A That   B Those   C These
8 _____ computer here is really slow.
  A That   B This   C These
9 Are _____ football players British?
  A this   B these   C that
10 Is _____ his pen?
   A these   B those   C this

6 ★★☆ **Complete the sentences with** *this, that, these* **or** *those.*

0 _____These_____ are the books I want, here.
1 _____ are my friends, over there.
2 _____ is my new phone, just here.
3 _____ are my new CDs, here.
4 _____ is my father, over there.
5 _____ is my bed, right here.
6 _____ are my cousins, there.
7 _____ is my brother's laptop, right there.
8 _____ are my DVDs, here.

GET IT RIGHT!
this and *these*

We use *this* to talk about singular objects that are near to us.
We use *these* to talk about plural objects that are near to us.
✓ **This** is my favourite dress.
✗ ~~These~~ is my favourite dress.
✓ **These** are my CDs.
✗ ~~This~~ are my CDs

Complete the sentences with *this* **or** *these.*

0 He gave me _____this_____ shirt.
1 Is _____ your pencil?
2 _____ are my favourite sweets.
3 I got _____ book yesterday.
4 Are _____ your computer games?
5 _____ are my old trainers.
6 I like _____ photo.

Pronunciation
this / that / these / those
Go to page 118.

VOCABULARY

Family members

MALE	FEMALE
son	daughter
father	mother
brother	sister
grandfather	grandmother
uncle	aunt
husband	wife
grandson	granddaughter
cousin	cousin

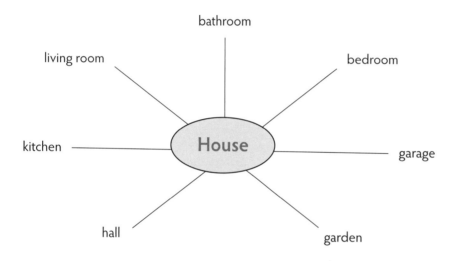

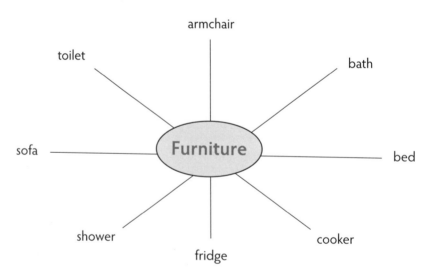

Key words in context

apartment	We live in an **apartment** on the 6th floor.
curtains	In my bedroom, there are green **curtains** on the window.
home	The house is very small, but it's my **home** and I love it.
photograph	I take great **photographs** with my new camera.
princess	She's the daughter of the king, so she's a **princess**.
queen	The UK and Denmark both have a **queen**.

Family members SB page 32

1 ★☆☆ **Complete the words.**

0 au _n_ _t_

1 _ o _

2 _ o _ _ e _

3 _ u _ a _ _

4 _ i _ e

5 _ o u _ i _

6 _ _ a _ _ o _ _ e _

7 _ _ a _ _ a _ _ e _

8 _ _ a _ _ _ o _

2 ★★☆ **Complete the puzzle. What's the mystery word?**

		O					
2			T				
3			S				
4				H			
5			E				
6			E				
7			G				

1 My _____ is forty-five; she's a teacher.

2 My _____ Julie is my mother's sister.

3 My little _____ is only five years old.

4 I'm twelve and my _____ is fourteen.

5 My _____ is from London. He's English.

6 My _____ Paolo is from Brazil.

7 Our teacher's _____ is in our class.

3 ★★★ **Write answers to the questions so they are true for you.**

1 Is your family big or small?

_____

2 What are your parents' names?

_____

3 How many cousins have you got?

_____

4 How many aunts and uncles have you got?

_____

5 Where do the people in your family live?

_____

6 How many people do you live with?

_____

House and furniture SB page 35

4 ★☆☆ **Circle the odd one out in each list.**

0	bath	shower	sofa
1	armchair	bedroom	kitchen
2	shower	hall	bathroom
3	cooker	bed	fridge
4	bedroom	garage	living room
5	garage	kitchen	garden
6	toilet	hall	kitchen

5 ★★☆ **Look at photos 1–5. Where in a house are these things? Write the words.**

0 _living room_

1 _____

2 _____

3 _____

4 _____

5 _____

6 ★★★ **Are these things in the correct place? Mark ✓ (yes, OK), ? (maybe) or ✗ (no).**

1 a shower in the garden ☐

2 a sofa in the bedroom ☐

3 a car in the garage ☐

4 a fridge in the bedroom ☐

5 a cooker in the garage ☐

6 a car in the hall ☐

7 a toilet in the bathroom ☐

8 an armchair in the garden ☐

READING

1 ▌REMEMBER AND CHECK▐ **Mark the sentences T (true) or F (false). Then look at the article on page 31 of the Student's Book and check your answers.**

0	Kate Middleton is English.	T
1	She likes playing football.	☐
2	Kate's family is from Scotland.	☐
3	She has a sister called Elizabeth.	☐

4	Kate is very famous now.	☐
5	William's grandfather is Prince Charles.	☐
6	She has a daughter called Ann.	☐
7	Kate's home is a small house.	☐

2 **Read the blog quickly. Is Mary Ann's family big or small?**

My family and I

Hi, everybody! This is the first post on my blog. I'm Mary Ann. I'm fourteen and I live in London. I have two brothers. Mark is twelve and Stephen is sixteen. My father is a teacher, but not at my school. Mum is from Canada and she works in London. She's a photographer for a newspaper.

I have a grandfather and grandmother in London and lots of aunts, uncles and cousins here, too. My mother's family are in Canada – her parents and her brother and sister. So I have family there, too. My favourite aunt is Polly. She's great and she's always nice to me. She's my father's sister.

Our house isn't big, but I have my own small bedroom. It's my favourite room in the house. I have photos and posters in my room and I have a table for my laptop and two chairs, and a bed, of course. Mark and Stephen's bedroom is big with two beds and a TV. They have a table and a shelf for their books and DVDs.

We also have a dog called Sport. He's Mark's pet. He's very big.
I have a cat. Her name is Smokey. She's my favourite.

Well, that's it for today. Please add your comments and questions.

3 **Read the blog again and complete the sentences with words from the text.**

0 Mary Ann has two ___brothers___ , Mark and Stephen.

1 Her father is a _____ .

2 Her mother is from _____ .

3 She's a _____ .

4 Mary Ann has family in _____ and in _____ .

5 Mary Ann's favourite aunt is called _____ .

6 Mary Ann's favourite room is her _____ .

7 Her brothers have two _____ and a TV in their room.

DEVELOPING WRITING

My bedroom

1 **Read the text. Find three or more differences between Jake's perfect bedroom and his real bedroom.**

> **My perfect bedroom and my real bedroom**
>
> My perfect bedroom is big. The walls are yellow and the floor is brown. The bed is very big – it's 2 metres long and 1.6 metres wide (I like big beds!). It's very comfortable, too, and it's the colour that my favourite football team plays in. So it's black and white because my favourite team is Juventus. The desk is near the window, with a comfortable chair for me to sit and work on my great new computer.
> My real bedroom isn't big. The floor is brown but the walls are blue. The bed is OK but it isn't very big and it isn't very comfortable! The bed is black and white – yay! My desk is near the door and the chair is small but it's OK. And I like my computer. It's old but it's really good!

2 **Complete the sentences with *and* or *but*.**

0 The walls are yellow ___*and*___ the floor is brown.

1 The bed is big _____ it's comfortable.

2 The bed is comfortable _____ it's in Real Madrid colours, too.

3 The computer is old _____ it's really good.

3 **Think about your perfect bedroom and about your real bedroom. Use the ideas below to help you make notes.**

	My real bedroom	My perfect bedroom
big / small?		
wall colour?		
floor colour?		
big / small bed?		
comfortable?		
bed colour?		
near the window?		
chair?		

4 **Use your notes to write about your real bedroom and your perfect bedroom.**

My real bedroom

My real bedroom _____ big. The floor is _____ and the walls are _____ . The bed is _____ . The bed is _____ . The _____ is near the window. The chair is _____ .

My perfect bedroom

My perfect bedroom _____ big. The floor is _____ and the walls are _____ . The bed is _____ . The bed is _____ . The _____ is near the window. The chair is _____ .

LISTENING

1 🔊 **18** Listen to the dialogue and complete the sentences. Write *Tony*, *Christine* or *Jack*.

0 _Christine_ says the room is nice.

1 _____ is Tony's brother.

2 _____ likes watching football.

3 _____ loves films.

4 The CDs are _____'s.

2 🔊 **18** Listen again and complete the words in this part of the dialogue.

CHRISTINE   Wow! Are these your DVDs, Tony?
They're ⁰g _reat_ !
I ¹l_____ films.

TONY   No, they're my brother's. He really
²l_____ old films. Very, very old films.

CHRISTINE   ³W_____ a ⁴n_____
collection!

TONY   Yeah. It's not bad. But the films are a bit
boring!

CHRISTINE   No, they're great! Hey! Are these your CDs?
They're ⁵f_____! This one
⁶i_____ really ⁷c_____!

TONY   Yeah, I ⁸r_____ ⁹l_____ Ella
Henderson. She's my favourite. She's a great
singer.

CHRISTINE   Let's listen to it now!

TONY   OK.

DIALOGUE

1 Put the dialogues in order.

Dialogue 1

☐ LUCY   Yes, it is cool. I love T-shirts!

1 LUCY   Happy birthday, Pat! This is a present for
you.

☐ LUCY   This one? It's from Italy. It's a birthday
present from my Italian friend.

☐ PAT   For me? Thanks, Lucy! Oh, a T-shirt! And it's
really cool!

☐ PAT   Your T-shirt's nice, too. I really like it.

Dialogue 2

☐ ALLY   Is your brother there, too?

☐ ALLY   Hi, Jim. Thanks. Wow, I really like your house.

☐ JIM   Thank you! Come into the kitchen. My mum
and dad are there.

1 JIM   Hi, Ally! Nice to see you. Come in!

☐ JIM   No, he's not. He's in his bedroom.

2 Look at Exercise 1 and complete the dialogues between you and a friend.

Dialogue 1

YOU   I really ¹*like* / *love* your T-shirt. Is it new?

FRIEND   Yes, it's from ²_____ .

YOU   It looks ³*great* / *nice* / *fantastic*.

FRIEND   Thanks.

Dialogue 2

YOU   What a ⁴*nice* / *great* / *fantastic* CD!

FRIEND   Yes, it's by ⁵_____ .

YOU   I really ⁶*like* / *love* it.

FRIEND   Let's listen to it now.

Dialogue 3

YOU   What a ⁷*fantastic* / *good* / *great*
computer game!

FRIEND   Yes. It's called ⁸_____ .

YOU   I really ⁹*love* / *like* computer games.

FRIEND   OK. Let's play it together!

3 Now write your own dialogue.

PHRASES FOR FLUENCY

SB page 37

1 ★☆☆ Complete the phrases with the missing vowels.

0 R e a lly?

1 _h, r_ght.

2 L_t's g_.

3 J_st _ m_n_t_.

2 Complete the dialogue with the phrases in the list.

just a minute | let's go | oh, right | ~~really~~

ANA   That boy over there is really nice.

JO   ⁰_Really_ ? Him? Well, he isn't my
favourite person.

ANA   I think he looks really cool.

JO   Well, he is, but sometimes he's difficult.

ANA   Hey, ¹_____ . Isn't he in your
family?

JO   Yes, he's my brother.

ANA   ²_____ . Your brother. OK.

JO   Ana, ³_____ ! We're late for class!

Sum it up

1 Look at the pictures and complete the crossword.

ACROSS

DOWN

2 Read the website about a famous house. Which of the things in the house is impossible to have?

Upton Abbey

⬤⬤⬤⬤◯

Come and visit Upton Abbey! This famous house is 400 years old. The Hogworth family live here – Lord Hogworth, Lady Hogworth and their four children.

Walk in the gardens! Walk round the house and visit its 20 bedrooms! And the 400-year-old kitchen – it's wonderful.

See ten fantastic old cars in the garage. See the 300-year-old fridge in the kitchen. See the old baths in the bathrooms. Everything here is old and different!

Open every weekend, 10.00–17.00, Friday, Saturday and Sunday. Only £10.00 per person or £25.00 for a family of three or more.

3 Complete the page from the website with information from the text.

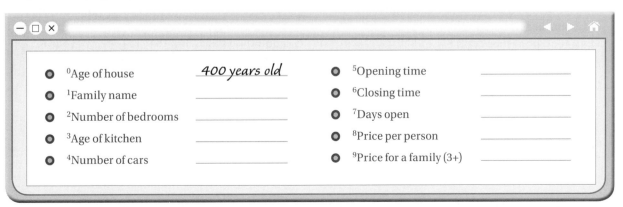

- ⁰Age of house   *400 years old*
- ¹Family name   _____
- ²Number of bedrooms   _____
- ³Age of kitchen   _____
- ⁴Number of cars   _____
- ⁵Opening time   _____
- ⁶Closing time   _____
- ⁷Days open   _____
- ⁸Price per person   _____
- ⁹Price for a family (3+)   _____

4 IN THE CITY

GRAMMAR

there is / there are SB page 40

1 ★☆☆ Complete the sentences with *is* or *are*.

0 There _____*are*_____ four bedrooms in the house.

1 There _____ two Brazilian girls at our school.

2 There _____ lots of famous squares in Paris.

3 There _____ a mountain near Tokyo called Mount Fuji.

4 _____ there a desk in your bedroom?

5 There _____ a small fridge in my parents' bedroom.

6 There _____ nine or ten big train stations in London.

7 There _____ eight people in my family.

8 _____ there any good shops here?

2 ★★☆ Complete the text with *there is*, *there isn't*, *there are* or *there aren't*.

> **Alice is 14. Here is what she says about Rosewood, her local shopping centre.**
>
> 'I really like our local shopping centre. It's small, but ⁰ *there is* a cinema. ¹_____ some cafés on the top floor, but ²_____ any restaurants. My mum likes it because ³_____ two good bookshops and ⁴_____ a great supermarket. My sister likes it because ⁵_____ some cool clothes shops. My brother doesn't like it because ⁶_____ a good sports shop (and he loves sport!). My dad doesn't like shopping.'

some / any SB page 40

3 ★☆☆ (Circle) the correct options.

0 There are (some) / any books in my room.

1 There aren't *some* / *any* good shops here.

2 There are *some* / *any* nice curtains in their house.

3 There aren't *some* / *any* interesting books in the library.

4 There aren't *some* / *any* banks in this street.

5 There are *some* / *any* fantastic things in the museum.

6 There aren't *some* / *any* cafés in the park.

7 There are *some* / *any* supermarkets in the town centre.

8 There are *some* / *any* chairs in the garden.

4 ★★☆ Complete the sentences with *some* or *any*.

0 There are _____*some*_____ good shops.

1 There aren't _____ sports shops.

2 There aren't _____ cinemas.

3 There are _____ computer shops.

4 There aren't _____ phone shops.

5 There are _____ cafés.

5 ★★☆ Complete the text with *there is a*, *there isn't a*, *there are some* or *there aren't any*.

> **Tim is 12. This is what he thinks of Parkland, his local shopping centre.**
>
> 'The shopping centre near my house is really big. There are about 400 shops in it. ⁰ *There is a* fantastic food hall. ¹_____ café with great ice creams. I like it because ²_____ good cinemas and a library, too. Mum says ³_____ good shoe shops, but they're not my favourite places. ⁴_____ DVD shop and ⁵_____ great music shops. The only bad things are that ⁶_____ computer shops and ⁷_____ restaurant.

6 ★★★ Complete the questions with *Is there a* or *Are there any*. Then look at the texts in Exercises 2 and 5 and answer the questions. Use *Yes, there is/ are.*, *No, there isn't/aren't.* or *I don't know.*

0   *Is there a*   supermarket in Rosewood?
    Yes, there is.

1   _____ cinemas in Rosewood?
    _____

2   _____ computer shop in Rosewood?
    _____

3   _____ clothes shops in Rosewood?
    _____

4   _____ sports shops in Rosewood?
    _____

5   _____ bank in Parkland?
    _____

6   _____ café in Parkland?
    _____

7   _____ library in Parkland?
    _____

8   _____ music shops in Parkland?
    _____

9   _____ restaurant in Parkland?
    _____

7 ★★★ Complete these sentences about a shopping centre you know.

1   There are _____ .
2   There aren't _____ .
3   There aren't _____ .
4   There are _____ .
5   There is _____ .
6   There isn't _____ .

Imperatives SB page 41

8 ★☆☆ (Circle) the correct options.

0   OK, everyone. Please (*listen*)/ *don't listen* to me. This is important.
1   Are you tired? *Go / Don't go* to bed late tonight.
2   Please *be / don't be* quiet in the library.
3   It's cold in here. *Open / Don't open* the window, please.
4   Hello. Please come in and *sit / don't sit* down.
5   Wow! *Look / Don't look* at that fantastic statue.
6   It's a very expensive shop! *Buy / Don't buy* your new clothes there!
7   To get to the cinema, *turn / don't turn* left at the supermarket, and it's there.
8   *Listen / Don't listen* to your brother. He's wrong.

9 ★★☆ Mick and Josh are looking for a sports shop. Complete the dialogue with the words in the list.

go | listen to | look | open | ~~sit down~~ | turn

MICK   Where's the sports shop?
JOSH   OK, [0] *sit down* on this chair and
        [1]_____ at the map.
MICK   I haven't got a map.
JOSH   Oh, well I've got an app.
MICK   Well [2]_____ the app on your phone, then.
JOSH   OK, OK. Wait a minute. Oh! Look, there's the sports shop. [3]_____ down here and [4]_____ left. The sports shop is behind the chemist's.
MICK   Is it opposite the phone shop?
JOSH   No, [5]_____ me again, Mick! It's on the corner, behind the chemist's.

GET IT RIGHT!

some and *any*

We use *some* in affirmative sentences and *any* in negative sentences.

✓ I've got **some** time.
✗ I've got ~~any~~ time.
✓ He hasn't got **any** money.
✗ He hasn't got ~~some~~ money.

Complete the sentences with *some* or *any*.

0   I haven't got   *any*   pets.
1   There are _____ good games.
2   Don't bring _____ food.
3   They haven't got _____ homework.
4   I have _____ time.
5   I have _____ presents for you.
6   We don't have _____ problems.

VOCABULARY

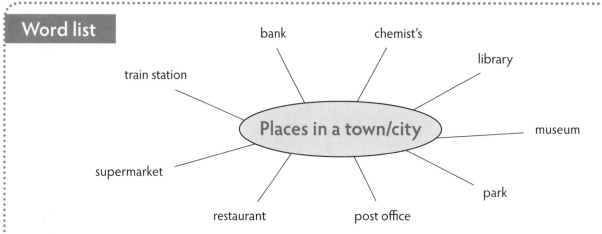

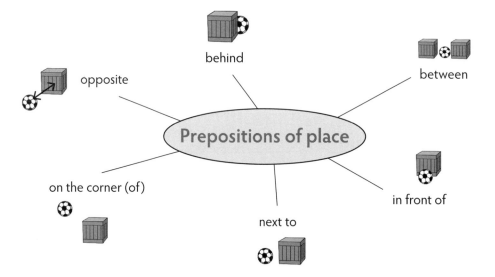

Numbers

one hundred and thirty	130
one hundred and fifty	150
one hundred and seventy-five	175
two hundred	200
five hundred and sixty	560
one thousand	1,000
one thousand two hundred	1,200
two thousand	2,000

Prices

dollar	$
pound	£
euro	€
nine pounds and ninety-nine	£9.99
twenty-one dollars and ninety-five cents	$21.95
seventy-two euros and fifty cents	€72.50

Key words in context

bookshop	This is a great **bookshop**. They've got books in different languages here.
expensive	That shirt is £150.00; it's very **expensive**!
famous	The Eiffel Tower in Paris is very **famous**.
palace	The king and queen live in that **palace**. It's got twenty bedrooms!
shoe shop	There's a new **shoe shop** in town. Their shoes are really nice!
square	St Peter's **Square** in Rome is very famous.
statue	There's a **statue** of a famous woman here.
tower	The BT **Tower** in London is 191 metres tall!

Places in a town/city SB page 40

1 ★★☆ **Where are these people? Write a word from the list.**

bank | chemist's | library | museum
park | ~~post office~~ | restaurant
supermarket | train station

0 Hi. This letter to Australia, please.
_____*post office*_____

1 Six apples and some bananas, please.
_____

2 Look! These things are 200 years old!
_____

3 A return ticket to Cambridge, please.
_____

4 Please be quiet in here. People are reading.
_____

5 It's a great day for a picnic here.
_____

6 Hi. Can I change these dollars for pounds, please?
_____

7 The steak and salad for me, please.
_____

8 I need some medicine for my eye.
_____

Prepositions of place SB page 41

2 ★☆☆ **Look at the map of the shopping centre and (circle) the correct options.**

0 The computer shop is *behind* / (*next to*) the bank.

1 The computer shop is *between* / *in front of* the bank and the bookshop.

2 The bookshop is *opposite* / *on the corner*.

3 The shoe shop is *between* / *opposite* the supermarket.

4 The bank is *next to* / *behind* the shoe shop.

5 The café is *behind* / *in front of* the cinema.

Pronunciation

Word stress in numbers

Go to page 119. 🔊

---

3 ★★☆ **Use the prepositions in Exercise 2 to complete the sentences.**

0 The chemist's is _____*next to*_____ the supermarket.

1 The restaurant is _____ the shoe shop.

2 The post office is _____ the restaurant and the phone shop.

3 The restaurant is _____ the supermarket.

4 The sports shop is _____ the chemist's.

5 The cinema is _____ the café.

6 The phone shop is _____ the bookshop.

Numbers 100+ SB page 42

4 ★☆☆ **Write the words or numbers.**

0 110 _____*one hundred and ten*_____

1 _____ one hundred and seventeen

2 125 _____

3 _____ one hundred and ninety-eight

4 215 _____

5 _____ three hundred and twelve

6 652 _____

7 _____ one thousand three hundred

8 1,400 _____

9 _____ two thousand six hundred and twenty

Prices SB page 43

5 ★★☆ **Write the prices in words.**

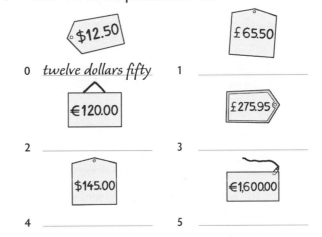

0 _*twelve dollars fifty*_ 1 _____

2 _____ 3 _____

4 _____ 5 _____

6 ★★★ **Write the name of places/things you know.**

1 a famous tower _____

2 a good shoe shop _____

3 a famous square _____

4 a statue of a famous person _____

5 a famous palace _____

READING

1 **REMEMBER AND CHECK** (Circle) the correct options. Then look at the brochure on page 39 of the Student's Book and check your answers.

0 Shenzhen is a (city)/ river.

1 Window of the World is in *China / Japan*.

2 It's a *museum / park*.

3 There are models of famous places from around *China / the world*.

4 You can take a ride on the *Hudson / Colorado* river.

5 China's national day is *January 1st / October 1st*.

6 There is a festival of *Chinese / pop* music every year.

7 There *are some / aren't any* restaurants in the park.

2 Read the emails quickly. Who lives in Australia?

From: Jack M

To: HarryP@mail.com

Subject: New home

Hi, Harry!

How are things in Sydney? Is it warm and sunny there? We're on holiday now and it's very cold and wet here in England. Nothing new there! December isn't my favourite month. There's some football on TV, but there are a lot of programmes about cooking and people dancing. There's a new café in town, but it's between a museum and the library. There are always a lot of old ladies in it – no young people.

I'm bored! Please email and tell me about Australia.

Jack

From: Harry P

To: JackM@mail.com

Subject: Re: New home

Hi, Jack!

Thanks for your email. I love it here. We're on holiday, too, but we're still in Sydney. And yes, it's very hot and sunny. There are some great beaches and lots of things to do. Our apartment isn't in the centre of town; it's opposite the beach! Sydney is fantastic. There are great cinemas and theatres, parks and, of course, Sydney Harbour Bridge and the famous Opera House. The bridge is beautiful, but opera isn't my favourite music. There are lots of great places to eat and some really cool cafés. My mum loves all the shopping centres.

Next email, all about my new school!!!!

Harry

---

3 Read the emails again. Mark the sentences T (true) or F (false).

0 It's December. | T |

1 Harry and Jack are on holiday. | |

2 There's a new shoe shop in Jack's town. | |

3 Jack loves the new café. | |

4 Harry lives in a house. | |

5 There are lots of cinemas in Sydney. | |

6 Harry's favourite music is opera. | |

7 Harry's mum likes the shopping centres. | |

8 Harry is at a new school. | |

DEVELOPING WRITING

Your town/city

1 Read the text. Does the writer like weekends in her town?

A weekend in my town

I like my town. It isn't very big but the people here are nice.

At the weekend, there are lots of things to do. The town centre is small but there are some nice shops and cafés, so I go into the centre on Saturday morning to meet my friends. We have coffee or a sandwich together, or we do some shopping. Some days we don't buy anything, but it's always fun.

There's a cinema in the town too, so on Saturday night or Sunday afternoon, my friends and I see a film together. I like football, so on Sunday morning I play with lots of friends in the park. There are three football pitches in the park. It's really good.

Not far from the town centre there is a river. It's great to swim there, but only in the summer!

My town is OK and my friends are great, so the weekends here are not bad.

2 Complete the sentences with *or*, *and* or *so*.

1 On Saturday evening we go to the cinema _____ we see a film.
2 Do you want to play football _____ volleyball?
3 My cousins live 300 kilometres away, _____ I don't visit them very often.

3 Match the words 1–3 with the phrases a–c.

1 in ☐
2 on ☐
3 at ☐

a the weekend
b the summer
c Sunday afternoon

4 Think about a weekend in your town/city. What do you do? Use the ideas below to help you make notes.

What I do on Saturday _____
_____
What I do on Sunday _____
_____
What I do with my friends _____
_____
What we do in summer _____
_____
What we do in winter _____
_____

5 Use your notes to complete the text.

Weekends in my town/city

I live in _____ . I _____ my town/city.
_____ the weekend I _____
Saturday morning. _____ Saturday afternoon I
_____ . On Sunday I _____ . With my
friends I _____ . _____ the summer
we _____ but _____ the winter we
_____ .

LISTENING

1 🔊20 **Listen to Stella and Matthew talking to their Aunt Mary. Tick (✓) the places they talk about.**

bank	☐
bookshop	☐
café	☐
chemist's	☐
library	☐
museum	✓
park	☐
post office	☐
shopping centre	☐
station	☐
supermarket	☐

2 🔊20 **Listen again and correct the sentences.**

0 There isn't a good shopping centre.
   There's a good shopping centre.

1 The museum is on Grand Parade.
   _____

2 The museum is very big.
   _____

3 The shopping centre is next to the museum.
   _____

4 Stella wants some pens and pencils for her project.
   _____

5 There aren't any cafés in the shopping centre.
   _____

6 Aunt Mary's favourite café is next to the bookshop.
   _____

DIALOGUE

1 **Stella is in a clothes shop. Put the dialogue in order.**

☐	WOMAN	£15.50.
☐	WOMAN	OK. That's £31.00, please.
1	WOMAN	Hello. Can I help you?
☐	WOMAN	Yes. There's this one here.
☐	STELLA	Hi. Yes. Have you got any yellow T-shirts?
☐	STELLA	Great! I'll take two, please.
☐	STELLA	Oh, it's really nice. How much is it?

2 **Complete the dialogue with the words and phrases in the list.**

~~Can~~ | expensive | is | much | That's | three

MAN	0 _____*Can*_____ I help you?	
MATTHEW	Yes, have you got any maps of the town?	
MAN	Yes, there are 1_____ different maps.	
MATTHEW	How 2_____ are they?	
MAN	They're £1.50 each.	
MATTHEW	OK, three, please.	
MAN	That's £4.50.	
MATTHEW	And how much 3_____ that small book about the museum?	
MAN	It's £5.70.	
MATTHEW	And that big book?	
MAN	That's £25.00.	
MATTHEW	That's very 4_____ . Just the maps and the small book.	
MAN	OK. 5_____ £10.20.	

3 **Imagine you're in a bookshop. Write a dialogue similar to the one in Exercise 1.**

_____
_____
_____
_____
_____
_____
_____
_____
_____
_____

▰ TRAIN TO THiNK ▰

Exploring numbers

Seth and John have to buy things for their room at home. They have £300. They buy five things and they have £35 left. Tick (✓) what they buy.

armchair – £60	☐
bed – £50	☐
chair – £20	☐
desk – £30	☐
DVD player – £25	☐
table – £35	☐
TV – £100	☐

EXAM SKILLS: Listening

Identifying text type

1 🔊21 **Listen to people talking in three different situations. How many people are speaking?**

Situation 1: _____

Situation 2: _____

Situation 3: _____

2 **Match the descriptions with the pictures. Write 1–3 in the boxes.**

1 a news report on TV

2 an announcement at a train station

3 people in a shop

3 🔊21 **Listen again. Match the situations with the pictures.**

Situation 1 → picture ☐

Situation 2 → picture ☐

Situation 3 → picture ☐

Listening tip

When you listen to a text for the first time, you don't need to understand every word.
Listen to the important things:

● Number of speakers.

● Sounds and noises to tell you where the speakers are.

● The way the speakers talk, e.g. are they happy, angry, worried, sad, excited, bored or none of these?

● 'Important' words – read the question first and think of words (nouns, adjectives or verbs) that might help you to answer it. These are 'important' words to listen for.

---

4 🔊21 **Listen again to the three situations. Which words helped you in Exercise 3?**

Situation 1: _____

Situation 2: _____

Situation 3: _____

CONSOLIDATION

LISTENING

1 🔊22 **Listen to Jeff talking about his family and where they live.** (Circle) **the correct answers (A, B or C).**

1 How many people are there in Jeff's family?

 A six   **B** eight   **C** ten

2 How many sisters has Jeff got?

 A four   **B** five   **C** six

3 Where is Jeff from?

 A the USA   **B** the UK   **C** Canada

4 What's his cousin called?

 A Paul   **B** Brad   **C** Clint

2 🔊22 **Listen again. How many are there? Write the numbers in the boxes.**

A

B

C

D

E

F

VOCABULARY

3 Match the words in A with the words in B to make pairs.

A

bathroom	uncle
living room	brother
son	kitchen
garage	husband

B

car	daughter
sofa	cooker
wife	sister
shower	aunt

0 *bathroom — shower*

1 _____

2 _____

3 _____

4 _____

5 _____

6 _____

7 _____

4 Name the shops and write the prices.

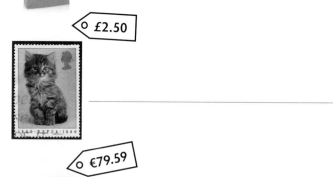

0 £3.29   *chemist's — It's three pounds twenty-nine.*

1 $14.99 _____

2 £2.50 _____

3 €79.59 _____

4 £12.99 _____

44

GRAMMAR

5 Complete the sentences with the words in the list. There are two extra words.

any | her | his | is | some | their | those | turn

1 Ask Luke. It's _____ sandwich.

2 There _____ a big park near my house.

3 Paul is Danny and Olivia's brother. He's _____ brother.

4 The shoe shop? OK, just _____ right on the High Street and it's there.

5 There aren't _____ parks near here.

6 Can I see _____ trousers in the window, please?

DIALOGUE

6 Complete the dialogue.

JORDAN   I like your T-shirt, Rachel.

RACHEL   [1]R_____ ? It's very old.

JORDAN   Well I think it [2]l_____ cool. And [3]w_____ a great hat, too.

RACHEL   [4]T_____ you. It's new.

JORDAN   How [5]m_____ was it?

RACHEL   Well, it was a present from my mum.

JORDAN   Oh, [6]r_____ . I'll ask her then.

READING

7 Read the dialogue and complete the sentences.

WOMAN	Hello, can I help you?
JEFF	Yes, I'd like to see those T-shirts behind you.
WOMAN	These red ones?
JEFF	No, the blues ones next to them.
WOMAN	OK. Yes, these are really nice. Here you are.
JEFF	How much are they?
WOMAN	Wait a minute. Let me see. They're £9.99.
JEFF	OK, can I have three, please?
WOMAN	Wow. You really like them.
JEFF	They're not for me. They're for my sisters.
WOMAN	Sisters?
JEFF	Yes. It's their birthday tomorrow.
WOMAN	So they're triplets?
JEFF	Yes, all three born on the same day.
WOMAN	Is it difficult? I mean having three sisters?
JEFF	Three! There's two more as well.
WOMAN	Five sisters! Poor you. Here, have another T-shirt for you.
JEFF	Wow, thanks. That's really kind.

1 Jeff wants to see the _____ T-shirts.

2 The T-shirts are _____ each.

3 The T-shirts are for his _____ .

4 It's their _____ tomorrow.

5 Triplets are _____ children born on the same day.

6 Jeff has _____ sisters.

7 The woman gives Jeff a free _____ .

8 Jeff thinks the woman is very _____ .

WRITING

8 Write a short text about your family and where you live. Write 35–50 words. Use the questions to help you.

- Who is there in your family?
- What is your house like?
- What is your town like?

5 IN MY FREE TIME

GRAMMAR
Present simple `SB page 50`

1 ★☆☆ (Circle) the correct options.

0 I (play) / plays tennis every day.

1 My brothers *speak* / *speaks* Spanish.

2 Mr Jones *teach* / *teaches* Maths.

3 The dog *like* / *likes* the park.

4 We sometimes *go* / *goes* to bed very late.

5 You *live* / *lives* near me.

2 ★★☆ Complete the sentences with the present simple form of the verbs in brackets. Which four sentences match with the pictures? Write the numbers in the boxes.

0 My dad ___*flies*___ planes. (fly)

1 The boys _____ a lot of video games. (play)

2 Miss Dawes _____ English. (teach)

3 Suzie _____ in the library every day. (study)

4 Tim and Dana _____ the guitar. (play)

5 Mum _____ flowers. (love)

A

B

C

D

3 ★★☆ Complete the sentences with the correct form of the verbs in the list.

finish | go | ~~like~~ | play | speak | study | teach | watch

0 Mum ___*likes*___ pop music.

1 My father _____ Music at my school.

2 Lucy _____ to a Glee club on Wednesdays.

3 Sam _____ four languages. He's amazing.

4 My brother _____ TV on Saturday mornings.

5 Our school _____ at 3.15 pm.

6 Gordon _____ the piano every day after school.

7 My sister _____ at a school in Birmingham.

Pronunciation
Present simple verbs – 3rd person
Go to page 119. 🔊

Adverbs of frequency `SB page 50`

4 ★☆☆ Put the adverbs in the correct order.

☐ often   [1] always   ☐ sometimes   ☐ never

5 ★★☆ Write the sentences with the adverb of frequency in the correct place.

0 I meet my friends in town on Saturdays. (sometimes)
   I sometimes meet my friends in town on Saturdays.

1 Jennie is happy. (always)
   _____

2 They do homework at the weekend. (never)
   _____

3 You help Dad make dinner. (sometimes)
   _____

4 We are tired on Friday afternoons. (often)
   _____

5 It rains on Saturdays! (always)
   _____

6 Mum flies to New York for work. (often)
   _____

7 I am bored in English lessons. (never)
   _____

6 ★★★ Write sentences so they are true for you. Use adverbs of frequency.

1 do homework after school

_____

2 play sport at the weekend

_____

3 watch TV on Sunday mornings

_____

4 listen to music in the morning

_____

5 phone my best friend in the evening

_____

Present simple (negative) `SB page 51`

7 ★★☆ Complete the sentences with the negative form of the verbs in brackets.

0 My mum _doesn't write_ books for children. (write)

1 I _____ to football lessons after school. (go)

2 My cousins _____ to a lot of music. (listen)

3 My dad _____ model planes. (make)

4 We _____ games on our tablet. (play)

5 School _____ at 8.15 am. (start)

6 My sister _____ singing or dancing. (like)

7 You _____ in a small house. (live)

8 ★★☆ Match these sentences with the sentences in Exercise 7.

0	0	She writes for teenagers.
a		It's really big.
b		But the gates open at that time.
c		We play them on the computer.
d		She's quite shy.
e		I go to them on Saturdays.
f		He makes trains.
g		But they watch a lot of TV.

Present simple (questions) `SB page 52`

9 ★☆☆ Complete the questions with do or does.

0 _Do_ you live in Manchester?

1 _____ Paul like sport?

2 _____ you know the answer?

3 _____ your sister play the piano?

4 _____ you often go to the cinema?

5 _____ your teacher give you a lot of homework?

10 Write the questions. Then write answers to the questions so they are true for you.

0 your mother / speak English?

Does your mother speak English?
Yes, she does.

1 you / always do your homework?

_____

_____

2 your best friend / play tennis?

_____

_____

3 you / sometimes play computer games before school?

_____

_____

4 you and your friends / play football?

_____

_____

5 your mum / drive a car?

_____

_____

GET IT RIGHT! 👁
Adverbs of frequency

With the verb *be*, we use this word order: subject + verb + adverb of frequency.

With other verbs, we use this word order: subject + adverb of frequency + verb.

✓ *He is always friendly.*
✗ ~~He always is friendly.~~
✓ *I often watch football on TV.*
✗ ~~I watch often football on TV.~~

Circle the correct sentences.

0 a I eat often pizza.
  (b) I often eat pizza.

1 a I go out often with friends.
  b I often go out with friends.

2 a I always go to the cinema with my friends.
  b Always I go to the cinema with my friends.

3 a Music is always great.
  b Music always is great.

4 a I play football in the park never.
  b I never play football in the park.

5 a I sometimes am bored.
  b I am sometimes bored.

VOCABULARY

Word list

Free-time activities

play computer games

dance

hang out with friends

go shopping

do homework

chat with friends online

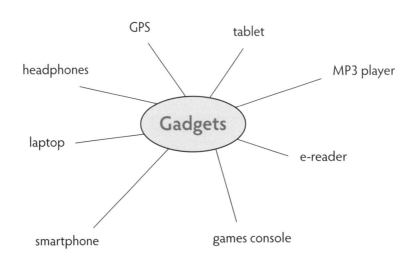

GPS · tablet · headphones · MP3 player · laptop · **Gadgets** · e-reader · smartphone · games console

Days of the week

MONDAY · TUESDAY · WEDNESDAY · THURSDAY · FRIDAY · SATURDAY · SUNDAY

Key words in context

carry	Don't **carry** all those books. They're very heavy.
cheer	I always **cheer** when my team scores a goal.
concert	I often go to pop **concerts** at the O2 stadium.
feel	I **feel** tired. I want to go to bed.
finish	School **finishes** at 4 pm.
fly	My mum **flies** planes for British Airways.
help	Dad often **helps** me with my homework.
meet	I sometimes **meet** my friends in the park at the weekend.
perform	My school **performs** a play every year.
sing	My dad always **sings** in the shower.
study	I **study** at St George's school.
teach	Mr O'Brian **teaches** Maths.

Free-time activities SB page 50

1 ★☆☆ **Match the parts of the sentences.**

0	I play	e
1	I go	☐
2	I hang out with	☐
3	I do	☐
4	I listen to	☐
5	I dance	☐

a   shopping with Dad on Saturdays.

b   my homework when I get home.

c   music in my bed.

d   to rock music in my bedroom.

e   computer games on my tablet.

f   my friends in the park on Sundays.

2 ★★☆ **Complete the sentences with the words in the list.**

dance | his homework | listens | ~~out~~
plays | shopping

0   Every day after school I hang ___out___ at the park.

1   Lucy goes _____ with her sister on Saturday mornings.

2   Tim never does _____ on time.

3   We _____ every weekend at the disco.

4   My brother _____ computer games all weekend!

5   My dad _____ to really old music!

3 ★★★ **Write sentences that are true for you. Use adverbs of frequency.**

1   play computer games

_____

2   go shopping

_____

3   dance

_____

4   do homework

_____

5   listen to music

_____

6   hang out with friends

_____

7   do sport

_____

8   go to the cinema

_____

Gadgets SB page 53

4 ★★☆ **Unscramble the letters to make words for gadgets.**

0	blteat	_tablet_
1	megas loscone	_____
2	P3M replay	_____
3	marsthopen	_____
4	ahehndspoe	_____
5	SGP	_____
6	plapto	_____
7	arae-der	_____

5 ★★★ **Answer the questions so they are true for you.**

1   Q What do you use to play computer games?
    A _____

2   Q What do you use to listen to music?
    A _____

3   Q What do you use to find your way?
    A _____

4   Q What do you use to read books, magazines or articles?
    A _____

Days of the week SB page 53

6 ★★☆ **Complete the days of the week with the missing letters. Then put the days in order.**

1	M o nday
☐	_ _ dnesday
☐	_ _ iday
☐	_ _ esday
☐	_ _ nday
☐	_ _ ursday
☐	_ _ turday

7 ★★★ **Choose three days. Write sentences so they are true for you.**

I love Fridays because I always go to the
cinema with my dad in the evening.

_____

_____

_____

_____

_____

READING

1 **REMEMBER AND CHECK** Complete the sentences with the missing words. Then look at the newsletter on page 49 of the Student's Book and check your answers.

0 The text is about a school *Glee* club.

1 People s_____ at these clubs.

2 Miss Higgins is a M_____ teacher.

3 They sing songs from f_____ .

4 They perform c_____ in front of the rest of the school three times a year.

5 The club is a good way to make f_____ .

6 The club is in the school h_____ .

7 They meet on Tuesdays and F_____ .

2 Look at the pictures and read the messages opposite. What rooms are these people in? What club are they in?

1 _____

2 _____

3 _____

4 _____

3 Match the sentences with the correct places (A–D) in the messages.

0 Tell your parents it finishes at 5 pm. ☐ *C*

1 (and some old songs, too). ☐

2 It's great for all students who love gadgets. ☐

3 Ask your parents about some of their favourites, and we can add them to the list. ☐

Computer gaming club

Come and get better at all your favourite games. Learn from your friends and show them what you know. Mrs Stephens also shows you how to make your own simple games.

A _____

Years 7 and 8 – Tuesday lunchtime in Room 4

• Dance club •

Join Mr Roberts for an hour of exercise and have loads of fun at the same time. Learn how to dance to all the best modern pop songs B_____ And it's not just for students at the school – anyone is welcome!'

All years – Wednesday lunchtime in the school gym

Homework club

Don't do all of your homework after school or at weekends. Come to Homework club and do it before you go home. When you get home after school you can have fun! C_____ There's always a teacher here to help you if you have a problem.

All years – Every day after school in Room 8

Film club

Watch classic films from the 1980s and 1990s *E.T., Toy Story, Jurassic Park* etc. Then talk about them with Miss Owens and other students. D_____ Bring your own popcorn!

Years 9–11, Thursday after school in Room 14

DEVELOPING WRITING

My week

1 **Read the text. On which day does Bruno not do any homework?**

POSTED: MONDAY 10 APRIL

Bruno's Busy Life

A typical week …

From Monday to Friday, I go to school from 9 am to 3 pm every day. But my day doesn't finish then!

After school on Mondays I have piano lessons from 4 pm to 5 pm. In the evenings I do my homework.

On Tuesdays and Thursdays I go to Tennis club from 4 pm to 6 pm. In the evenings I do my homework.

On Wednesday afternoons I go to Dance club from 3 pm to 4 pm. And in the evenings? Yep, I do my homework.

On Fridays I do my homework after school! I go to Glee club in the evenings. It finishes at 9 pm.

On Saturdays I do things with Mum and Dad. We go shopping or visit Grandma. My dad sometimes takes me to watch the football.

On Sundays I sleep! Oh, and then I do some homework.

2 **Complete the sentences with the correct prepositions. Use the text in Exercise 1 to help you.**

1 I play tennis _____ Tuesdays and Thursdays. I play _____ 4 pm _____ 6 pm.

2 _____ Wednesday afternoons I go to Dance club. It starts _____ 3 pm and finishes _____ 4 pm.

3 _____ Monday to Friday I go to school.

3 **Match the parts of the phrases. Then check your answers in the text in Exercise 1.**

1 do ☐
2 go ☐
3 have ☐

a a tennis lesson
b to Dance club / shopping
c homework

4 **Think about your life. Use the questions to make notes about the things you do.**

What do you do in the day?

_____

What do you do in the evening?

_____

What do you do at the weekend?

_____

5 **Use your notes to complete the text so it is true for you.**

A typical week …

From Monday to Friday I go to school. _____ every day! But my day doesn't finish then.

After school on Mondays I _____ .
In the evenings _____ .
On Tuesdays _____ .
In the evenings _____ .
On Wednesdays _____ .
In the evenings _____ .
On Thursdays _____ .
In the evenings _____ .
On Fridays _____ .
In the evenings _____ .
On Saturdays _____ .
On Sundays _____ .

LISTENING

1 🔊24 **Listen and put the events in order.**

	a	Jane feels better.
	b	Jane tells her mum about the singing.
	c	Jane tells her mum the name of the song.
	d	Jane tells her mum the name of the play.
1	e	Jane is unhappy.
	f	Mum starts playing the piano.

2 🔊24 **Listen again and correct the sentences.**

0 Jane is in the school tennis team.

Jane is in the school play.

1 Jane likes acting and singing.

_____

2 Jane thinks she's a good singer.

_____

3 The song is from *The Lion King*.

_____

4 Mum is a good piano player.

_____

DIALOGUE

1 **Complete the dialogue with the phrases in the list.**

don't worry | here to help you | No problem
You can do this | ~~You're good~~

JANE	Yes, my character is Elsa! She sings a lot in the play. And I'm a terrible singer.
MUM	You aren't. ⁰ _You're good_ . Just like me.
JANE	Really?
MUM	Yes, really. Come on. ¹_____ .
JANE	I can?
MUM	Yes, you can. And I'm ²_____ .
JANE	You are?
MUM	Yes, ³_____ . Now what's the song?
JANE	It's `Let it Go' from the film.
MUM	⁴_____ . Come with me to the piano.

2 **Look at the picture and write a short dialogue. Use phrases from Exercise 1.**

PHRASES FOR FLUENCY SB page 55

1 **Match the sentences.**

0	What's wrong?	*d*
1	I've got an idea.	
2	Ana, do you want to be in the school tennis team?	
3	I don't want to play football.	

a Really. What is it?
b No way!
c Oh, come on. We really need you.
d I feel a bit ill.

2 **Use two of the pairs of sentences in Exercise 1 to complete the dialogues.**

Dialogue 1

GEORGE _____

SARA _____

GEORGE But I hate football. And I'm terrible at it.

SARA No, you're not. You're great.

Dialogue 2

ABI I'm sorry, Simon. I don't really want to go shopping.

SIMON _____

ABI _____

SIMON Oh, dear. Let me get you a glass of water.

3 **Use the other two pairs of sentences in Exercise 1 to make your own dialogues.**

Sum it up

1 This is Lucy's diary. Make sentences about her week.

0 *On Monday she goes shopping.*

1 _____

2 _____

3 _____

4 _____

5 _____

MONDAY	shopping
TUESDAY	dance
WEDNESDAY	friends
THURSDAY	computer games
FRIDAY	homework
SATURDAY	music
SUNDAY	sleep!

2 Use the code to work out the message.

CODE

♋ = a	♌ = b	♍ = c	♎ = d
♏ = e	♐ = f	♑ = g	♒ = h
♓ = i	ℰ𝓇 = j	& = k	● = l
○ = m	■ = n	□ = o	⬜ = p
▫ = q	❒ = r	◆ = s	◆ = t
◆ = u	❖ = v	◆ = w	⊠ = x
⬓ = y	⌘ = z		

3 What do you want? Use the code to write your own message.

_____

_____

_____

6 | FRIENDS

GRAMMAR
have / has got (positive and negative)
SB page 58

1 ★☆☆ (Circle) the correct options.

0 I *has got* / (*have got*) a new friend.

1 My friend, Sam, *has got* / *have got* a tablet.

2 Jenny *has got* / *have got* a big family.

3 We *has got* / *have got* a cat.

4 All of my friends *has got* / *have got* bikes.

2 ★★☆ Look at the table and complete the sentences.

has / hasn't got	Sally	Tom	Dan	Ellie
smartphone	✓	✗	✓	✗
laptop	✗	✗	✗	✗
bike	✓	✗	✓	✓
TV	✗	✓	✗	✗
dog	✓	✓	✓	✓

0 Tom *hasn't got* a smartphone.

1 Sally _____ a laptop or a TV.

2 Dan and Ellie _____ a bike.

3 Tom _____ a TV.

4 All of them _____ a dog.

5 Tom and Dan _____ a laptop.

3 ★★★ Write sentences so they are true for you. Use *have got* or *haven't got* and the phrases in the list.

a big family | a new phone number
a new smartphone | a sister | a tablet
black hair | brown eyes | three brothers

1 _____

2 _____

3 _____

4 _____

5 _____

6 _____

7 _____

8 _____

4 ★★★ Write sentences under the pictures. Use the phrases in the list and *have got* or *has got*.

a shaved head | long curly hair
long straight hair | short curly hair

have / has got (questions) SB page 59

5 ★☆☆ (Circle) the correct options.

1 A (*Have*) / *Has* you got a TV in your bedroom?

   B No, I *haven't* / *hasn't*. But my brother has got one.

2 A *Have* / *Has* Katy got a friendship band?

   B No, she *haven't* / *hasn't*. She doesn't like them.

3 A *Have* / *Has* Jake and Andy got new mobile phones?

   B No, they *haven't* / *hasn't*. But I *have* / *has* got one.

4 A *Have* / *Has* you got lots of songs on your mobile?

   B Yes, I *have* / *has*. I've got thousands. I listen to them all the time.

5 A *Have* / *Has* you got bikes?

   B Yes, we *have* / *has*. We've both got bikes. We ride to school every day.

6 A *Have* / *Has* Simon got a sister?

   B No, he *haven't* / *hasn't*. He's got a brother.

6 ★★☆ Complete the dialogue with the correct form of *have got*.

JANE   0   _Has_   your mum   _got_   brown hair?

MARCUS   No, she 1_____. She 2_____ black hair.

JANE   3_____ she _____ blue eyes?

MARCUS   No, she 4_____. She 5_____ green eyes.

JANE   6_____ she _____ a daughter?

MARCUS   No, she 7_____. She 8_____ one son – me!

7 ★★★ Complete the dialogue about a member of your family.

FRIEND   Has he/she got green eyes?

YOU   _____

FRIEND   Has he/she got a big family?

YOU   _____

FRIEND   Has he/she got a car?

YOU   _____

FRIEND   Has he/she got a dog?

YOU   _____

FRIEND   Has he/she got a smartphone?

YOU   _____

Countable and uncountable nouns
SB page 59

8 ★☆☆ Write C (countable) or U (uncountable).

0	chair	C	5	time	☐
1	nose	☐	6	work	☐
2	hair	☐	7	hospital	☐
3	fun	☐	8	name	☐
4	friend	☐	9	teacher	☐

9 ★★☆ Circle the correct options.

0 It's the weekend. Let's have *a /* (*some*) fun.

1 I've got *a / some* sandwiches. I'm hungry. Let's eat one.

2 Let's listen to *a / some* music on your smartphone.

3 Marie's got *a / some* red bike.

4 I've got *a / some* money. Let's buy an ice cream.

5 He's got *a / some* hobby – painting!

6 My dad's got *a / some* work to do.

7 Murat hasn't got *an / some* apple. He's got *a / some* banana.

10 ★★☆ Complete the dialogues with *a*, *an* or *some*.

1 A   Would you like _____ *some* _____ ice cream?

   B   No, thanks. I've got _____ apple.

2 A   Have you got _____ hobby?

   B   Yes, I have. I sing in a band.

3 A   Have you got _____ best friend?

   B   Yes, I have. Her name's Zeynep.

4 A   I've got _____ money from my mum.

   B   Me too!

   A   That's good. Let's buy _____ sweets.

5 A   I haven't got a pen.

   B   Oh, I've got _____ . I've got blue, black and red. Is that OK?

   A   Yes, perfect!

GET IT RIGHT!
Countable and uncountable nouns

We add *-s* to the end of countable nouns to make them plural, but not to uncountable nouns.

✓ I have a lot of **friends**.

✗ I have a lot of ~~friend~~.

✓ I drink a lot of **water**.

✗ I drink a lot of ~~waters~~.

Circle the correct options.

0 How many *pen /* (*pens*) has he got?

1 I listen to *musics / music* in my bedroom.

2 They have a lot of *hobby / hobbies*.

3 Do you have enough *money / moneys* for your lunch?

4 Homework isn't always a lot of *fun / funs*.

5 Her brother has two *phone / phones*.

6 This street has a lot of *shop / shops*.

VOCABULARY

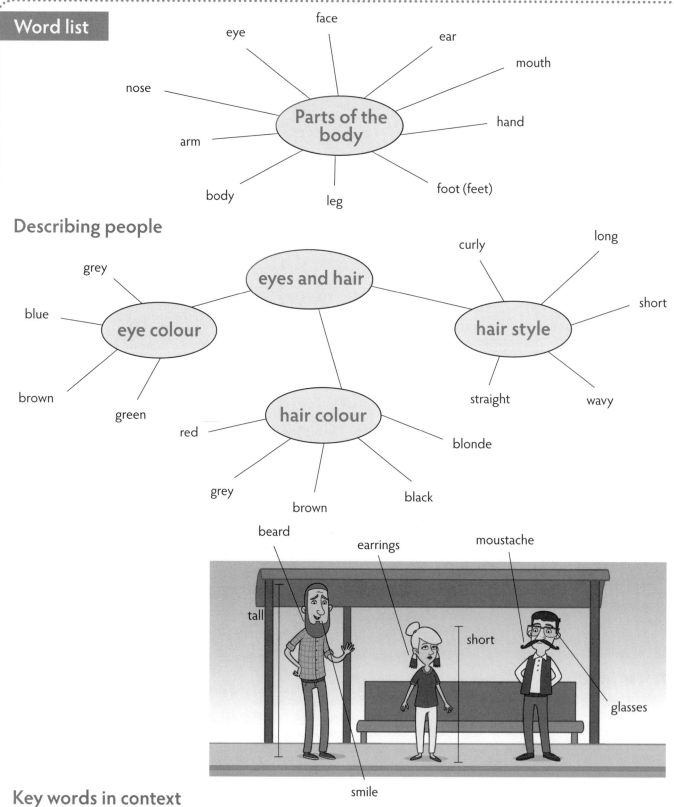

Parts of the body
- eye
- face
- ear
- mouth
- nose
- hand
- arm
- body
- leg
- foot (feet)

Describing people

eyes and hair

eye colour
- grey
- blue
- brown
- green

hair style
- curly
- long
- short
- straight
- wavy

hair colour
- red
- grey
- brown
- black
- blonde

- beard
- earrings
- moustache
- tall
- short
- glasses
- smile

Key words in context

doctor	When I'm ill, I see a **doctor**.
good-looking	James has got black hair and blue eyes. He's very **good-looking**.
kiss	When we greet a friend in my country, we **kiss** three times on the cheeks.
nurse	My mum is a **nurse** at a hospital.
shaved	My dad hasn't got any hair. He's got a **shaved** head.
surprise	I've got a present for Jane. It's a **surprise**.
tradition	I always eat cake on my birthday. It's a **tradition**.

Parts of the body SB page 58

1 ★☆☆ Complete the crossword.

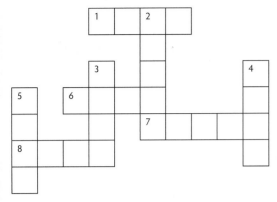

ACROSS
1 You reach with your _____ .
6 You kick with your _____ .
7 You hold with your _____ .
8 You hear with your _____ .

DOWN
2 You eat with your _____ .
3 You walk with your _____ .
4 You smell with your _____ .
5 You see with your _____ .

Describing people (1) SB page 60

2 ★★☆ Circle the correct options.

0 His hair isn't curly. It's *wavy* / *brown*.
1 She's got *short* / *blonde* red hair.
2 Her eyes are *straight* / *green*.
3 My mother always wears her hair *straight* / *brown* for work.
4 The old man has grey *curly* / *hair*.
5 His hair *colour* / *style* is black.

Describing people (2) SB page 61

3 ★☆☆ Complete the words with *a, e, i, o* or *u*.

0 m o u s t a c h e
1 gl _ ss _ s
2 t _ ll
3 b _ _ r d
4 sm _ l _
5 _ _ rr _ ngs
6 sh _ rt

4 ★★☆ Match the words to the pictures. Write 1–6 in the boxes.

1 beard | 2 earrings | 3 glasses | 4 grey
5 moustache | 6 wavy

5 ★★★ Look at the picture and write the names of the people.

0 She's got earrings. _Seline_
1 He's got a very big moustache. _____
2 She's got a lovely smile. _____
3 He's got a very long beard. _____
4 She wears glasses. _____

6 ★★★ Write one more sentence about each person in Exercise 4.

1 _____
2 _____
3 _____
4 _____

Pronunciation

Long vowel sound /eɪ/

Go to page 119.

READING

1 REMEMBER AND CHECK Mark the sentences T (true) or F (false). Then look at the article on page 57 of the Student's Book and check your answers.

0 Delaney Clements is 12. | F |
1 Delaney has got long curly hair and blue eyes. | □ |
2 She loves sports. | □ |
3 Kamryn is her best friend. | □ |
4 Delaney has got cancer. | □ |
5 Delaney shaves her head. | □ |

2 Read the two dialogues about friendship and answer the questions.

1 Who has got green eyes? _____

2 Who wears glasses? _____

JANET   Who is your best friend?

CLARA   Sarah is my best friend.

JANET   What does she look like?

CLARA   She's very pretty. She's got long curly black hair and brown eyes. She wears glasses and she's got a friendly smile.

JANET   What's she like?

CLARA   She's very clever and she's very kind. She likes drawing and making things. I like making things, too. We've got the same hobbies. That's important, I think.

JANET   Why is she a good friend?

CLARA   Friends share things with you. Sarah shares everything with me. She shares her chocolate with me and her clothes with me. She's a very special friend.

JANET   Who is your best friend?

SAM   Murat is my best friend.

JANET   What does he look like?

SAM   He's tall and he's got short straight brown hair and green eyes. He's got a friendly smile and he laughs a lot. We laugh a lot together. We like the same things.

JANET   What's he like?

SAM   He's funny and tells good jokes. He's very good at sports, and he likes basketball. I like basketball, too. We like the same team. That's important, I think.

JANET   Why is he a good friend?

SAM   Friends listen to you. Murat always listens to me. Sometimes I have a problem and he helps me. He's a great friend.

3 Read the dialogues again and answer the questions.

1 What colour is Sarah's hair?   _____
2 What colour is Murat's hair?   _____
3 Who likes basketball?   _____
4 Who likes drawing?   _____
5 What do Murat and Sam like?   _____
6 What does Sarah share with Clara?   _____

4 Who says these phrases about friendship? Write C (Clara) or S (Sam).

A good friend …

1 □ shares things with you.
2 □ likes the same team.
3 □ helps you.
4 □ has the same hobbies.
5 □ tells you jokes.
6 □ listens to you.

DEVELOPING WRITING

Describing people in a story

1 Read about a singer from a story.
Mark the sentences T (true) or F (false).

1 He's short. ☐
2 He wears glasses. ☐
3 He's got a moustache. ☐
4 He hasn't got a beard. ☐
5 He doesn't like tennis. ☐

In my story, there's a singer. He's in a boy band. He's very tall. He's got short black hair and blue eyes and he wears glasses. He's got a short beard. I think he's very good-looking. He's very active. He likes football and swimming, but he doesn't like tennis. He's very friendly. Look! He's got a big smile. I think he's cool.

2 Think of a person from a story. He/She can be a singer, a sports person, an actor/actress, a prince/princess, etc. Choose the adjectives that describe him or her.

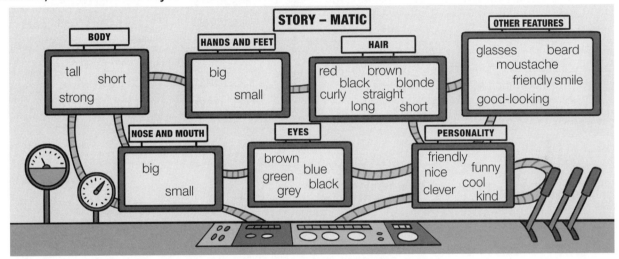

STORY – MATIC

BODY
tall short
strong

HANDS AND FEET
big small

HAIR
red brown
black blonde
curly straight
long short

OTHER FEATURES
glasses beard
moustache
friendly smile
good-looking

NOSE AND MOUTH
big small

EYES
brown
green blue
grey black

PERSONALITY
friendly
nice funny
clever cool
kind

3 Write notes about your story person. Use the questions to help you.

What does he/she look like? (hair, eyes, other features) _____

_____

Personality _____

_____

Likes/dislikes _____

4 Use your notes to complete the text about your story person.

In my story, there is a/an _____ .
He/She is _____ . He/She has got
_____ and _____ .
He/She has also got _____ and
_____ . And what about his/her
personality? He/She is _____
and _____ . He/She likes
_____ but he/she doesn't like
_____ .
I like him/her very much.

Writing tip: adjectives to describe people

- He/She is *tall / short*.
- He/She has got *long / black / curly* hair.
- He/She has got *brown / blue / green* eyes.
- He/She has got a *black / grey / brown / long / short moustache / beard*.
- He/She is *nice / friendly*.

LISTENING

1 🔊27 **Listen to the dialogues and number the places in the order you hear them.**

a ☐ the park

b ☐ a hospital

c ☐ a party

2 🔊27 **Listen again and ⟨circle⟩ the correct options.**

1 Martin is *tall / short* and he's got short curly *brown / black* hair. He's got a *moustache / friendship band* and he wears *glasses / earrings*.

2 Katie has got a *dog / bike* with her. She's *short / tall* and she's got long curly *brown / black* hair. She's got *brown / blue* eyes and she always wears *glasses / earrings*. She's very *funny / friendly*.

3 The nurse is *tall / short* and she's got *short / long* hair. It's *black / blonde* and it's *curly / straight*. She's got *brown / green* eyes and she's very *popular / pretty*.

DIALOGUE

1 Put the dialogue in order.

☐	POLICE OFFICER	And what's your daughter's name?
☐	POLICE OFFICER	And what colour eyes has she got?
1	POLICE OFFICER	Can I take your name?
☐	POLICE OFFICER	Thank you, Mrs Jones.
☐	POLICE OFFICER	OK, first, what colour hair has she got?
☐	POLICE OFFICER	Is it long or short?
☐	MRS. JONES	She's got brown hair.
☐	MRS. JONES	My name's Sarah Jones.
☐	MRS. JONES	She's got green eyes and she wears glasses.
☐	MRS. JONES	It's Emma.
☐	MRS. JONES	It's short and curly.

▰▰ TRAIN TO THiNK ▰▰▰

Attention to detail

Spot the five differences and write sentences.

Picture 1

Picture 2

0 *In picture 1, the man has got glasses.*
In picture 2, he hasn't got glasses.

1 _____

_____

2 _____

_____

3 _____

_____

4 _____

EXAM SKILLS: Writing

Punctuation (getting apostrophes right)

Writing tip

When writing in English, it's sometimes easy to make mistakes with apostrophes ('). It's important to know when to use them and when not to use them.

- We use apostrophes to show missing letters in short forms, for example:

  He is … → He's …

  She has got … → She's got …

- Be careful not to confuse apostrophes for the short form of *be* and *have got* with apostrophes to show possession:

  My mum's got curly hair. (short form)

  My mum's name is Helen. (possession)

1 Complete the *Apostrophe Challenge*. Write the short forms.

I think I can complete the *Apostrophe Challenge* in _____ seconds.

I am	**0**	*I'm*
It is	**1**	
You are	**2**	
He is not	**3**	
They are not	**4**	
She has got	**5**	
I have got	**6**	
We have got	**7**	
He has not got	**8**	
I have not got	**9**	

My time: _____ seconds.

2 Read the text. Put apostrophes in the correct places.

> My best <u>friends</u> name is Miranda. Shes
>
> 12 years old and shes in the same class
>
> as me. Mirandas got short curly brown
>
> hair and green eyes. She wears glasses
>
> and shes very pretty. Shes clever and she
>
> likes sports. Mirandas got a brother and
>
> a sister. Theyre eight years old and ten
>
> years old. Theyve got brown hair and blue
>
> eyes. They dont wear glasses. Mirandas
>
> also got a cat. Its black and white and its
>
> names Suky. Its a lovely cat.

3 Write a paragraph about one of these people. Use the questions in the box to help you.

a   your best friend

b   a family member

c   your favourite actor/singer/band

- What's his/her name?

- How old is he/she?

- What does he/she look like?

CONSOLIDATION

LISTENING

1 🔊 **28** Listen to three dialogues and (circle) the correct answers (A, B or C).

1 Jonathan has got a problem with his …
   A arm.   B hand.   C leg.

2 Maddy is …
   A nice.   B short.   C tall.

3 How many friends has Tim got?
   A about fifty   B about fifteen   C about five

2 🔊 **28** Listen again and answer the questions.

1 What does Jonathan want to do today?

_____

2 What does the girl tell him to do?

_____

3 Does Mike know Maddy?

_____

4 What does Mike want Samantha to say to Maddy?

_____

5 When does Tim come to this place?

_____

6 What colour is Steve's hair?

_____

GRAMMAR

3 (Circle) the correct options.

TOM   Hi Joanna. How are you? It's nice to see you here.

JOANNA Hi Tom. Well, I ¹*go always / always go* to the shopping centre on Saturdays.

JASON   Oh, right. ²*I'm never / I never am* in town on Saturdays. But it's different today because ³*I've got / I'm got* some money.

JOANNA Great. ⁴*How much / How many* money have you got, then?

TOM   £75.00. I ⁵*don't know / know not* what I want to buy, though. Maybe some clothes, or … .

JOANNA That's a great idea. I love clothes. I ⁶*buy / buys* clothes every month.

TOM   Really? So, ⁷*you got / you've got* lots of clothes at home?

JOANNA Yes, that's right.

TOM   OK, well I'm not very good at buying clothes. Can you help me? Have you got ⁸*a / some* time to come with me?

JOANNA Of course. Let's go to this shop first – ⁹*it's always got / it's got always* nice things to buy.

TOM   OK, cool. You know, Joanna, it's great to have ¹⁰*a / some* friend like you!

VOCABULARY

4 Complete the sentences with the words in the list. There are two extra words.

do | earrings | e-reader | eyes
hang out | headphones | legs
short | smile | tall

1 I really like listening to music with my
   _____ .

2 Spiders have got eight _____ .

3 I like Susannah. She's always happy and she's got a nice _____ .

4 These are my new _____ . Do you like them?

5 I don't buy books any more. I've got an _____ .

6 She's good at basketball because she's very _____ .

7 I only _____ my homework on Sundays – never on Saturdays!

8 On Sundays I always _____ with my friends.

5 Complete the words.

1 My favourite day of the week is
   F _ _ _ _ _ _ .

2 I use my new t _ _ _ _ _ _ every day to check my emails and things.

3 Her hair isn't straight. It's c _ _ _ _ _ .

4 Let's go out on W _ _ _ _ _ _ _ _ _ evening – to the cinema, maybe?

5 My grandfather's got a b _ _ _ _ _ and a moustache.

6 His eyes aren't very good. He wears g _ _ _ _ _ _ _ all the time.

7 Do you want to go s _ _ _ _ _ _ _ _ in town tomorrow morning?

8 Put your h _ _ _ up if you know the answer.

DIALOGUE

6 **Complete the dialogue with the words in the list.**

always | an idea | haven't got | listen to | never | on | play | tablet | way | wrong

PAUL   Hey, Jenny. You don't seem very happy. What's ¹_____ ?

JENNY   Hi, Paul. I'm OK. It's nothing.

PAUL   Come ²_____ . Tell me. Is there a problem?

JENNY   No, not really. I want to ³_____ computer games tonight, but I ⁴_____ anyone to play with.

PAUL   OK. Listen. I've got ⁵_____ . Let's ask James to come over to my place. Then we can all play some games together.

JENNY   No ⁶_____ ! I don't like James at all. He ⁷_____ helps me or says anything nice to me. He's ⁸_____ horrible to me.

PAUL   Oh, right, OK. So – let's play, you and me. I'm not very good, but …

JENNY   Oh, yes, please. That's great, Paul. Thank you. So – can we use your laptop?

PAUL   Sorry, Jenny, I haven't got a laptop. But I've got a ⁹_____ . Is that OK?

JENNY   Yes, I think so. And we can ¹⁰_____ music at the same time, too.

PAUL   Sure. OK, let's go.

READING

7 **Read this text about gadgets and (circle) the correct answers (A or B).**

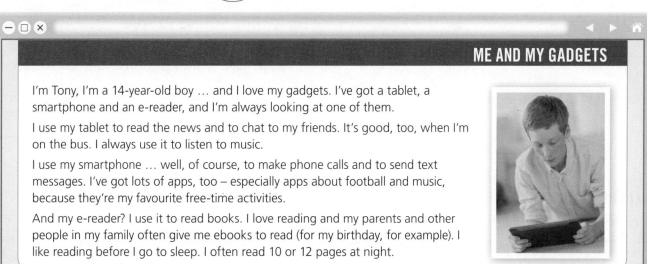

ME AND MY GADGETS

I'm Tony, I'm a 14-year-old boy … and I love my gadgets. I've got a tablet, a smartphone and an e-reader, and I'm always looking at one of them.

I use my tablet to read the news and to chat to my friends. It's good, too, when I'm on the bus. I always use it to listen to music.

I use my smartphone … well, of course, to make phone calls and to send text messages. I've got lots of apps, too – especially apps about football and music, because they're my favourite free-time activities.

And my e-reader? I use it to read books. I love reading and my parents and other people in my family often give me ebooks to read (for my birthday, for example). I like reading before I go to sleep. I often read 10 or 12 pages at night.

1 Tony's got …
   A three gadgets.
   B four gadgets.

2 He listens to music on …
   A his smartphone.
   B his tablet.

3 Tony uses his smartphone to …
   A read about the news and weather.
   B talk to his friends.

4 People in Tony's family often give him …
   A ebooks for his reader.
   B pages from books to read at night.

WRITING

8 **Write a paragraph about your gadgets. Use the questions to help you. Write 35–50 words.**
   ● What gadgets have you got?
   ● What do you use them for?
   ● When / How often do you use them?
   ● What gadgets do you want?

PRONUNCIATION

UNIT 1
/h/ or /w/ in question words

1 Look at the question words. Two of them start with the /h/ sound and the others start with the /w/ sound. Write /h/ or /w/ next to the words.

0 Why   /w/
1 How
2 Where
3 Who
4 What
5 When

2 ◀》10 Listen, check and repeat.

3 Match the words that sound the same.

0 Why   a now
1 How   b got
2 Where   c chair
3 Who   d then
4 What   e l
5 When   f you

4 ◀》11 Listen, check and repeat.

UNIT 2
Vowel sounds – adjectives

1 ◀》13 Listen and repeat the adjectives.

angry	awful	bored	busy
friendly	funny	happy	hot
hungry	sad	thirsty	worried

2 Complete the table with the words in Exercise 1.

a (cat)	e (get)	i (six)	o (dog)
0 *angry*	3	4	5
1			
2			

u (bus)	or (for)	ir (bird)	
6	9	11	
7	10		
8			

3 ◀》14 Listen, check and repeat.

UNIT 3
this / that / these / those

1 ◀》17 Listen and repeat. Then look at the underlined sounds and circle the odd sound out.

0	those	go	home	bored
1	that	sad	late	have
2	them	these	please	meet
3	give	like	this	sing
4	hot	cold	know	those
5	wife	this	nice	exciting
6	these	she	get	we
7	famous	that	family	happy

2 ◀》17 Listen again, check and repeat.

UNIT 4
Word stress in numbers

1 🔊19 Listen to the words and write them in the correct column according to the stress.

eighteen | eighty | forty | fourteen | nineteen
ninety | sixteen | sixty | thirty | thirteen

oO	Oo
eighteen	eighty

2 🔊19 Listen again, check and repeat.

UNIT 5
Present simple verbs – 3rd person

1 Complete the table with the correct present simple third person singular form of the verbs in the list.

catch | cook | choose | dance | help | look
sing | teach | walk | wash | watch | wish | work

One syllable	Two syllables
cooks	catches

2 🔊23 Listen, check and repeat.

UNIT 6
Long vowel sound /eɪ/

1 🔊25 Listen to these words. They all contain the /eɪ/ sound. Underline the sound in each word.

0 br<u>ea</u>k
1 eight
2 face
3 great
4 grey
5 make
6 rainy
7 say
8 straight
9 take
10 they
11 waiter

2 Complete the sentences with the words in Exercise 1.

0 How do you _____say_____ that word in English?

1 Is your grandmother the woman with the wavy _____ hair?

2 Let's _____ Clara a friendship band for her birthday!

3 My little sister is _____ years old.

4 These are my friends. _____ like playing football with me.

5 It's _____ today. Let's go to the cinema.

6 My father's a _____ at that restaurant.

7 I brush my teeth and wash my _____ every morning.

8 I like playing tennis. It's a _____ game!

9 Can you _____ this book to your teacher? Thank you.

10 My hair's _____ but my best friend's hair is curly.

11 Put your books away. It's time for a _____ .

3 🔊26 Listen, check and repeat.

GRAMMAR REFERENCE

UNIT 1
Question words

1. **Questions that begin with *Who* ask about a person / people.**

   Who is he?
   He's the new teacher.

2. **Questions that begin with *What* ask about a thing / things.**

   What's that?
   It's a mobile phone.

3. **Questions that begin with *When* ask about a time / day / year / etc.**

   When's the football match?
   It's at three o'clock.

4. **Questions that begin with *Where* ask about a place.**

   Where's Cambridge?
   It's in the UK.

5. **Questions that begin with *Why* ask for a reason.**

   Why are you here?
   Because I want to see you.

6. **Questions that begin with *How old* ask about age.**

   How old is she?
   She's sixteen.

to be

1. **The present simple of *to be* is like this:**

Singular	Plural
I am	we are
you are	you are
he/she/it is	they are

2. **In speaking and informal writing we use contracted (short) forms.**

   I'm, you're, he's, she's, it's, we're, they're

   I'm from Russia.

   She's late.

   We're hungry.

UNIT 2
to be (negative, singular and plural)

1. **We make the verb *to be* negative by adding *not*.**

Singular	Plural
I am not (I'm not)	we are not (we aren't)
you are not (you aren't)	you are not (you aren't)
he/she/it is not (he/she/it isn't)	they are not (they aren't)

   I'm not Brazilian. I'm Portuguese.
   He isn't late. He's early!
   They aren't from Spain. They're from Mexico.

to be (questions and short answers)

To make questions with *to be*, we put the verb before the subject. We make short answers with *Yes* or *No* + subject + the verb *to be*. We don't use contracted forms in positive short answers (NOT: *Yes, you're.*)

Am I late?	Yes, you are. / No, you aren't.
Are you American?	Yes, I am. / No, I'm not.
Is he a singer?	Yes, he is. / No, he isn't.
Is she from Japan?	Yes, she is. / No, she isn't.
Are we right?	Yes, we are. / No, we aren't.
Are they French?	Yes, they are. / No, they aren't.

Object pronouns

1. **Object pronouns come after a verb. We use them instead of nouns.**

   I like the film. I like it.
   I love my sister. I love her.
   They are friends with you and me. They are friends with us.
   I like the girls at my school. I like them.

2. **The object pronouns are:**

Subject	I	you	he	she	it	we	they
Object	me	you	him	her	it	us	them

UNIT 3
Possessive 's

1 We use 's after a noun to say who something belongs to.

Dad's room
John's car
Sandra's family
the cat's bed
my brother's friend
your sister's school

2 We don't usually say ~~the room of Dad, the car of John~~, etc.

Possessive adjectives

1 We use possessive adjectives before a noun to say who something belongs to.

My name's Joanne.
Is this your pen?
He's my brother. I'm his sister.
She's nice. I like her smile!
The cat isn't in its bed.
We love our house.
Are the students in their classroom?

2 The possessive adjectives are:

Subject pronoun	I	you	he	she	it	we	they
Possessive adjective	my	your	his	her	its	our	their

this / that / these / those

1 We use *this* or *these* to point out things that are close to us. We use *that* or *those* to point out things that are not close to us, or are close to other people.

Look at this photograph – it's my sister.
These oranges aren't very nice.
That shop is a really good place for clothes.
We don't like those boys.

2 We use *this* or *that* with a singular noun. We use *these* or *those* with plural nouns.

this photograph   *that* house
these rooms   *those* tables

UNIT 4
there is / there are

1 *There is (There's)* and *There are* are used to say that something exists.

There's a small shop in our street.
There are two supermarkets near here.
There are lots of great shops in the town centre.

2 *There's* is the short form of *There is*. In speaking and informal writing, we usually say *There's*.

3 In positive sentences, we use *there's* with a singular noun and *there are* with plural nouns.

There's a cat in the garden.
There's an old lady in the café.
There are nice shops in this street.

4 In questions and negative sentences, we use *a/an* with a singular noun and *any* with plural nouns.

Is there a bank near here?   *There isn't a bank near here.*
Are there any restaurants here? *There aren't any restaurants here.*

some / any

1 We use *some* and *any* with plural nouns.

There are some good films on TV tonight.
There aren't any games on my tablet.

2 We use *some* in positive sentences. We use *any* in negative sentences and questions.

There are some nice trees in the park.
There aren't any places to play football here.
Are there any good shoe shops in the town?

Imperatives

1 We use the imperative to tell someone to do something, or not to do something.

Come here!
Don't open the door!

2 The positive imperative is the same as the base form of the verb.

Turn right.
Open the window, please.

3 The negative imperative is formed with *Don't* and the base form of the verb.

Don't listen to him – he's wrong!
Don't open the window – it's cold in here.

UNIT 5
Present simple

1 The present simple is used to talk about things that happen regularly or are usually true.

I go to school at 8 o'clock every day.
She watches TV after school.
We play the piano.
They love chocolate.

2 The present simple is usually the same as the base form, but we add -s with 3rd person singular (he/she/it).

I like pizza.   *He likes pizza.*
They live in London.   *She lives in London.*

3 If the verb ends with o, sh, ch, ss, z or x, we add -es.

go – he goes   finish – it finishes   catch – she catches
miss – it misses   fix – he fixes

4 If the verb ends with a consonant + -y, the y changes to i and we add -es.

carry – it carries   study – he studies   fly – it flies

5 If the verb ends with a vowel + -y, it is regular.

buy – she buys   say – he says

Adverbs of frequency

1 Adverbs of frequency tell us *how often* people do things. Adverbs of frequency include:

always   usually   often   sometimes   hardly ever   never

100%   0%

2 Adverbs of frequency come after the verb *be*, but before other verbs.

I'm always hungry in the morning.
I usually have breakfast at 7.00.
He's often tired.
He sometimes goes to bed early.
They're never late.
They hardly ever go on holiday.

Present simple (negative)

The present simple negative is formed with *don't (do not)* or *doesn't (does not)* + base form of the verb.

I don't play tennis.
She doesn't play football.
My grandparents don't live with us.
My brother doesn't live with us.

Present simple (questions)

Present simple questions are formed with *Do / Does* + subject + base form of the verb.

Do you like the film?   *Does Mike like shopping?*
Do I know you?   *Does she know the answer?*
Do your friends play video games?   *Does your dog play with a ball?*

UNIT 6
have / has got (positive and negative)

1 The verb *have/has got* is used to talk about things that people own.

I've got a bicycle. (= There is a bicycle and it is my bicycle.)
He's got a problem. (= There is a problem and it is his problem.)

2 We use *have got* with *I/you/we/they*. We use *has got* with *he/she/it*. In speaking and informal writing, we often use the short forms: *'ve got / 's got*.

My mother's got black hair and blue eyes.
My friends have got a nice cat.
We've got two fridges in our kitchen.

3 The negative form is *hasn't / haven't got*.

I haven't got a tablet.
This town hasn't got a park.
They haven't got a car.

have / has got (questions)

We make questions with *Has/Have* + subject + *got*. Short answers use *has/have* or *hasn't/haven't*. Remember that we don't use contracted forms in positive short answers (e.g. NOT: *Yes, I've.*)

Have you got my book?   Yes, I *have*.
Has your father got brown hair?   Yes, he *has*.
Has the shop got any new DVDs?   No, it *hasn't*.

Countable and uncountable nouns

Nouns in English are countable or uncountable.

1 Countable nouns have a singular and a plural form. We can count them. We use *a/an* with the singular nouns. We can use *some* with the plural nouns.

He's got a house.   *He's got two houses.*
There's a picture on my wall.   *There are six pictures on my wall.*
There's an orange in the fridge.   *There are some oranges in the fridge.*

2 Uncountable nouns are always singular – they haven't got a plural form. We can't count them. We can use *some* with uncountable nouns.

I like music.   *Let's listen to some music.*
I like Japanese food.   *Let's eat some Japanese food.*

3 We don't use *a/an* or numbers with uncountable nouns.

NOT ~~a bread~~   ~~an information~~   ~~three works~~

IRREGULAR VERBS

Base form	Past simple
be	was
begin	began
buy	bought
can	could
catch	caught
choose	chose
come	came
do	did
draw	drew
drink	drank
drive	drove
eat	ate
fall	fell
feel	felt
find	found
fly	flew
get	got
give	gave
go	went
have	had
hear	heard
keep	kept
know	knew
learn	learnt/learned
leave	left

Base form	Past simple
light	lit
make	made
meet	met
pay	paid
put	put
read /riːd/	read /red/
ride	rode
run	ran
say	said
see	saw
send	sent
sing	sang
sit	sat
sleep	slept
speak	spoke
stand	stood
take	took
teach	taught
tell	told
think	thought
understand	understood
wake	woke
wear	wore
write	wrote

Acknowledgements

The authors and publishers acknowledge the following sources of copyright material and are grateful for the permissions granted. While every effort has been made, it has not always been possible to identify the sources of all the material used, or to trace all copyright holders. If any omissions are brought to our notice, we will be happy to include the appropriate acknowledgements on reprinting.

Corpus

Development of this publication has made use of the Cambridge English Corpus (CEC). The CEC is a computer database of contemporary spoken and written English, which currently stands at over one billion words. It includes British English, American English and other varieties of English. It also includes the Cambridge Learner Corpus, developed in collaboration with Cambridge English Language Assessment. Cambridge University Press has built up the CEC to provide evidence about language use that helps to produce better language teaching materials.

English Profile

This product is informed by the English Vocabulary Profile, built as part of English Profile, a collaborative programme designed to enhance the learning, teaching and assessment of English worldwide. Its main funding partners are Cambridge University Press and Cambridge English Language Assessment and its aim is to create a 'profile' for English linked to the Common European Framework of Reference for Languages (CEF). English Profile outcomes, such as the English Vocabulary Profile, will provide detailed information about the language that learners can be expected to demonstrate at each CEF level, offering a clear benchmark for learners' proficiency. For more information, please visit www.englishprofile.org

Cambridge Dictionaries

Cambridge dictionaries are the world's most widely used dictionaries for learners of English. The dictionaries are available in print and online at dictionary.cambridge.org. Copyright © Cambridge University Press, reproduced with permission.

The publishers are grateful to the following for permission to reproduce copyright photographs and material:

T = Top, B = Below, L = Left, R = Right, C = Centre, B/G = Background

p. 5 (TL): Peshkova / Getty Images; p. 5 (TL): © Michael Dwyer / Alamy; p. 5 (TL): © Rrrainbow / Alamy; p. 5 (TL): © Zoonar GmbH / Alamy; p. 5 (TL): Foodcollection / Getty Images; p. 5 (TL): © RTimages / Alamy; p. 5 (TL): © The Picture Pantry / Alamy; p. 5 (TL): fStop Images / Getty Images; p. 5 (TL): © Tetra Images / Alamy; p. 5 (TL): © YAY Media AS / Alamy; p. 5 (TL): vsl / Shutterstock; p. 5 (BL): © Ivan Vdovin / Alamy; p. 5 (BL): © Tom Grundy / Alamy; p. 5 (BL): © Tetra Images / Alamy; p. 5 (BL): © russ witherington / Alamy; p. 5 (BL): © Nadiya Teslyuk / Alamy; p. 6 (TR): Jose Luis Pelaez Inc / Getty Images; p.

6 (BR): © TongRo Images / Alamy; p. 7 (TL): koya79 / Getty Images; p. 7 (TL): © Archideaphoto / Alamy; p. 7 (TL): © RTimages / Alamy; p. 7 (TL): Datacraft Co Ltd / Getty Images; p. 7 (TL): © Dmitry Rukhlenko / Alamy; p. 7 (TL): Hemera Technologies / Getty Images; p. 7 (TL): © Anton Starikov / Alamy; p. 7 (TL): © aviv avivbenor / Alamy; p. 7 (BL): © Héctor Sánchez / Alamy; p. 7 (BL): © Zoonar GmbH / Alamy; p. 7 (BR): © Robert Fried / Alamy; p. 7 (BR): Siri Stafford / Getty Images; p. 10 (BL): © Radius Images / Alamy; p. 11 (BL): filipefrazao / Getty Images; p. 11 (BL): © PHOVOIR / Alamy; p. 11 (BL): © wareham.nl (sport) / Alamy; p. 11 (BL): © E.D. Torial / Alamy; p. 11 (BL): © Zoonar GmbH / Alamy; p. 11 (BL): STOCK4B/ Getty Images; p. 13 (TR): © wiba / Alamy; p. 13 (TR): © HolgerBurmeister / Alamy; p. 14 (CR): © James Davies / Alamy; p. 14 (CR): AFP / Getty Images; p. 15 (TR): Kali Nine LLC / Getty Images; p. 15 (TR): Kali Nine LLC / Getty Images; p. 15 (TR): omgimages / Getty Images; p. 16 (TL): Laurence Cartwright Photograph/ Getty Images; p. 16 (TL): © Bloomimage/Corbis; p. 16 (TL): Juanmonino/ Getty Images; p. 16 (TL): © Tetra Images / Alamy; p. 16 (TL): PeopleImages.com / Getty Images; p. 17 (TL): Kai_Wong / Getty Images; p. 17 (TL): Lya_Cattel/ Getty Images; p. 17 (TL): Thierry Levenq / Getty Images; p. 17 (TL): © Horizon Images/Motion / Alamy; p. 19 (TL): © Imagestate Media Partners Limited - Impact Photos / Alamy; p. 22 (CR): © ZUMA Press, Inc. / Alamy; p. 24 (TL): © age fotostock / Alamy; p. 27 (CL): Ron Levine / Getty Images; p. 27 (TL): © Katrina Brown / Alamy; p. 27 (TR): Hill Street Studios / Getty Images; p. 31 (CR): © Archideaphoto / Alamy; p. 31 (CR): © Y H Lim / Alamy; p. 31 (CR): Charlie Dean / Getty Images; p. 31 (CR): Christopher Steer / Getty Images; p. 31 (CR): PhotoAlto / Laurence Mouton / Getty Images; p. 31 (CR): Maciej Toporowicz, NYC/ Getty Images; p. 32 (TR): © Eric Audras/Onoky/Corbis; p. 37 (TR): Paul Bradbury / Getty Images; p. 40 (TR): © Image Source / Alamy; p. 41 (TR): © OJO Images Ltd / Alamy; p. 44 (BR): © Danny Smythe / Alamy; p. 44 (BR): flyfloor / Getty Images; p. 44 (BR): satori13/ Getty Images; p. 44 (BR): © Art Directors & TRIP / Alamy; p. 44 (BR): © Y H Lim / Alamy; p. 51 (TR): © Victorio Castellani / Alamy; p. 51 (TR): John Rowley/ Getty Images; p. 54 (TR): Andresr / Shutterstock; p. 54 (TR): © debbiewibowo / RooM the Agency / Corbis; p. 54 (TR): © Beau Lark/Corbis; p. 54 (TR):© Image Source / Corbis; p. 55 (TR): Tetra Images / Getty Images; p. 59 (TR): Luna Vandoorne / Shutterstock; p. 61 (BL): © Radius Images / Alamy; p. 63 (BR): Tetra Images / Getty Images.

Cover photographs by: (L): ©Tim Gainey/Alamy Stock Photo; (R): ©Yuliya Koldovska/Shutterstock.

The publishers are grateful to the following illustrators:

Christos Skaltsas (hyphen) 6, 8 (L), 10, 26, 28, 35 (L), 38, 39 (R), 43, 46, 50, 52, 56, 57, 59, 60 and Zaharias Papadopoulos (hyphen) 8 (R), 12, 16, 20, 35 (TR), 39 (L), 44, 48, 58.

The publishers are grateful to the following contributors:

hyphen: editorial, design and project management; Leon Chambers: audio recordings; Karen Elliott: Pronunciation sections; Matt Norton: Get it right! exercises